# *Dancing* With

# Change

~

# HUGH WILEY

Hujo Press

Published by Hujo Press


National Library of Canada Cataloguing in Publication

Wiley, Hugh, 1937-
    Dancing with change: create your life
in 3 proven steps / Hugh Wiley.

ISBN 0-9730963-0-6

    1. Change (Psychology). 2. Self-actualization
(Psychology). I. Wiley, Joanne, 1949-  II. Title.
BF637.C4W54 2002   158.1  C2002-902536-2

~

Edited by Betsy Brierley
Design by Warren Clark
Proofread by Lynne Betts
Cover Photograph
© Alec Pytlowany/Masterfile

Printed and bound in Canada

To Joanne

whose love, support, and belief in me

made this book possible

~

## Acknowledgments

I am deeply grateful to clients, associates, and friends, some of whose stories are included in this book. They have allowed me my mistakes and shared their own. They have pointed out my wisdom as they shared theirs with me. Where I have described their experiences in the book, I've altered information to ensure confidentiality. All names and any information that would identify people have been changed—to the extent of combining stories—so that any similarity to someone you know is coincidental. They all have contributed to my dance of life.

I appreciate Ann and Gary Deatherage, Dave Lyons, Kate Hall, John Roshak, Fred Dubray, Serena Naeve, and Judy McAdam for their unwavering faith in my professional skills. It was Ann who said, "Well, Hugh, I guess you'll just have to write a book." I am very grateful to Duane Holden, Jim Miller, Diane Bonneau, Kathryn Gray, Dan Cook, Carol Breen, Doreen Douglas, Ruth Johnson, Dick Bonnycastle, Barry Foster, Ruth Floyd, and Allan Markin, who all shared themselves and encouraged my growth. Naturally, the list is much more extensive and there are many more people whom I thank for their profound effect on my life.

I found writing a book requires the talents and cooperation of many others. Thank you Kris Hoglund, Lynne Betts, and Warren Clark for generously contributing your talents and abilities. I give special thanks to my editor, Betsy Brierley, who was unstinting in her pursuit of brevity and clarity, while always excelling in diplomacy.

List of Exercises

# Chapter 1

# Chapter 2

# Chapter 3

# Chapter 4

# Chapter 5

# Chapter 7

# Contents

Introduction

# Introduction

If you want that wonderful feeling that you are directing changes in your life, read on. If you have experienced a devastating event, if you want to design your own transitions, read on.

This book encourages you to shift from resisting change to welcoming it. You'll learn how to master the process of transition using a simple step-by-step procedure. Dancing with change, you'll glide past blocks and barriers to achieve what you really want.

Have you ever thought of viewing change as an opportunity for growth, rather than associating it with loss? It is the association with loss that causes you pain and prompts you to resist change. This book shows you how to overcome this resistance and release your pain. For those of you who have worn out countless pairs of shoes dragging your feet, this book helps you switch to dancing shoes.

This "how-to book" guides you through unsatisfying life situations so that you can optimize them into growth opportunities. If you are experiencing changes in career, business, a personal relationship, or the transitions of aging and retirement, you will find the information in this book addresses your needs. It is, however, *not* intended to replace professional therapy. If you feel you are in need of this type of counseling, I strongly recommend you pursue it.

The uniqueness of this book lies in its useful, practical approach to change. Regardless of your circumstances, you will discover simple methods for leading a more satisfying life in which you utilize your talents and special abilities to reap rewards. I have included numerous examples from my own experiences and those of clients and associates. You learn that achieving successful change is not limited to a gifted few. Success is possible for anyone.

Change has many times broken the continuity of my life. My parents separated when I was ten. At age sixteen, I graduated from high school and started work as a laborer because there was no money to continue my schooling. Through many ensuing changes, I became a psychologist and a successful businessman, returning eventually to practise my profession. My experience in the field of psychology ranges from college counseling, industrial psychology, management training and corporate planning to counseling in private practice. These experiences taught me that mastery of change is necessary to achieve what I desire in life. My many career moves put me in contact with associates and clients who demonstrated how to transform uninvited events into opportunities. They gave me a deep appreciation of how to evolve through the change process. The techniques and strategies they used are detailed in these pages.

My personal life has been equally packed with change. I have been faced with separation and divorce and have entered new relationships. I have been blessed with the responsibility of raising children and stepchildren. These rich experiences have yielded the insight that nothing is fixed, and miracles are often a normal part of life. Utilizing this book chapter by chapter, you will find what you previously thought was impossible in your life can become a reality.

Fear, the largest hurdle, hampers many of us in adapting to change. This book explains how to transform fear into energy for action. It guides you to direct that energy and lays down the necessary foundation to support your efforts. During the journey from where you are to where you want to be, there is no need to experience that "lost" feeling. Exercises and step-by-step procedures show you how to achieve your desires and enjoy the process. Your fear transforms to excitement and enthusiasm, creating for you a different life with enhanced meaning and satisfaction.

Chapter 1 identifies the characteristics of change. By learning what to look for, you recognize that change is your ally rather than an enemy. Understanding that you can change only yourself gives new insights to your responsibilities. You then can claim freedom to express yourself and share your talents and skills with the world. This chapter describes how to find your power, allow your "wants," and appreciate the value of stability in the midst of change.

Chapter 2 explains the reactions you have when you experience change that is imposed on you. The fear and the feeling of being victimized are explored so that you can master the accompanying anger, denial, and resistance. Rather than seeing this type of change as a setback or misfortune, you learn how to turn it into an opportunity. You are directed how to deal with the anxiety that generates when you are confronted with the unknown and how to manage worries, doubts, and guilt.

Chapter 3 teaches you how to become a visionary. Your vision is so important that the change process can be described in three steps: create your vision, believe your vision, and allow it to happen. This section gives you the tools to uncover your long-forgotten dreams and use them to chart the direction you want your life to take. You now lead in the dance of life.

In Chapter 4, you discover how your beliefs form your world and how they trap or free you. If you are trapped, you learn a process to identify the beliefs that are holding you prisoner so you can bring them under your control. You then develop a strategy to change these beliefs so that they serve you rather than limit you.

Chapter 5 shows you how to develop the necessary support system to follow through to your goals. You discover your true worth and how your worth matches your desires.

The actual process of change—the action phase—is discussed in chapter 6. Here you are guided to your goal. Following the steps provided puts you in the present moment so you don't fall prey to the pitfalls of past and future worries.

Chapter 7 presents the solution when you feel blocked or stymied. It steers you back on course or helps you seek a different path if it's appropriate.

You will use your natural ability to adapt and make changes with the numerous exercises and examples. By reawakening your appreciation of your uniqueness and your responsibility to express that uniqueness, life becomes a dance. You lead, choosing your experiences as partners. You respond to life's events by gliding around obstacles that appear before you. In this great dance of life, you move easily to your dreams, enjoying each amazing step.

Chapter 1

# Learning the Dance Steps:
# What You Need to Know about Change

"I am always standing on the brink of tomorrow knowing what happens is up to me," Burt reflected. "How do I make this good life better?" Burt owned a multimillion-dollar trucking firm with fifty employees. "At one time I cringed thinking of tomorrow," he went on. "Now I welcome it!"

At sixteen, Burt dropped out of school with a grade nine education. He felt unwanted at home and was already involved with the law. One day, looking to see what he could steal off a truck, he instead helped the trucker put chains on his rig. The trucker bought Burt a cup of coffee, then hired him as his helper—a "swamper" in trucker language. Burt became a driver, later bought his truck and eventually his own company. Burt definitely knew how to dance with change; now he wished to learn some new steps. He felt constrained by his lack of education, yet he doubted that he was capable of attending university. He sought me out to sort through his puzzle.

Burt knew change was inevitable.

## You are a change-master

Change *is* inevitable. The only option you have is how you deal with it. Change is something that you dread, or welcome, or it's somewhere in between—a mixed bag.

Change is natural. Would you have liked to remain as you were at three years old, or ten, or twenty? I am sure the answer is no! There have been tremendous physical changes you have adapted to and would not reverse. And look at all the emotional and mental adjustments you have made since your teen years. Look at the career and professional changes you have accomplished. Without realizing it, you have become a master of change.

When you look back, you will note that some changes were difficult; others were easy. The difference is a function of how much you resisted each of these shifts. When you resist change, you find that often you feel tired and overwhelmed. You get worn down trying to keep things constant in your life. When you do not resist, things flow naturally, and you are able to take advantage of the new you. When you fight change, it is a time of scrambling and catch-up. Stress and worry are signs of unhappiness you experience when you resist change.

Holden came to see me experiencing this frustration. He was feeling lost and confused in his relationship with his wife, Donna. She had moved from being a dependent mother and housewife to an assertive businesswoman. She was now selling real estate and making an income that sometimes exceeded Holden's. His complaint was: "She is not the woman I married." I agreed with him that this was probably true. We then examined the changes he had made since their marriage. He found that he was not the same man Donna had married, that he was a very different person, too! Recognizing this gave him a basis to start a new relationship with his wife.

Meeting with both Donna and Holden, I went on to explore with them how they had changed since their wedding day. Much of their marital frustration was coming from trying to relate to partners who existed only in the past. Once they realized that the people they were fifteen years ago no longer existed, they started accepting some of the changes each had made. The relationship became much fuller and more meaningful as they each accepted the "new person" as their partner.

Accepting that change is inevitable is most necessary. Giving yourself and others permission to grow is critical. It negates the guilt feelings of deception and betrayal that sneak in when you make personal changes that impact on your relationships. There is a pressure or a sense that you should not behave in a different way, that any changes you make should have the approval of the other party. You get the idea that change should only be done in lockstep and with their approval. This control restricts your growth and is a waste of your uniqueness. Unless you express your inner beauty, your uniqueness, which I call your *divinity*, it's difficult to justify your existence. What purpose do you serve if you don't express your real self? Mirroring the values of other members of the family deprives them, and the world, of experiencing you. True deception occurs when you claim to be an individual, yet express yourself as a mirror image of others.

## Experience liberation

By accepting that change is inevitable, you then approach it with a different mindset, a fresh perspective. Rather than viewing change as a restriction, look upon it as liberation. Here is an opportunity that offers you new experiences and the possibility to express another aspect of you. In the case of Holden and Donna, Holden initially felt attacked and restricted. He felt there was little of his wife's personality he could still relate to, or that he felt familiar with. When he accepted the changes she had made, he found new opportunities to relate to her and to express himself. He actually was liberated to demonstrate different aspects of himself, which allowed him to lead a more satisfying life and freed Donna to express herself more openly and fully.

Prior to Holden's insight, he was sending messages laden with guilt and judgment to his wife. The ideas he was entertaining about himself were not positive either. Relaxing his resistance had a truly positive effect on the couple. The irony was that they both had adapted to the changes that had occurred but had not given themselves permission to accept them. When you grant yourself permission to change or to accept the changes that have resulted, it is liberating.

## Upshift your life

You don't have to be wrong to make changes. The basis for a change is to create a shift, to improve your life. You want to instill more meaning, to give more, and to experience more of your potential. This is an important aspect of the process of change. When you contemplate a change, the action is usually cloaked in an aura of correcting some deficit. There has to be something wrong with you, or why would you be considering alterations? To approach change this way is disempowering.

It is also one of the most inopportune times to judge yourself. Change is stressful, and the additional burden of feeling wrong makes it more difficult to take the necessary action. So the next time you consider making a change in your life, approach it as something you want to do, something you want to accomplish.

That is precisely how I quit smoking. I had attempted to quit many times, but it wasn't until I changed my attitude on smoking that I was successful. Instead of judging myself wrong to be a smoker, I saw myself wanting to be a non-smoker. Rather than dissipating my energy by criticizing myself, I was able to praise myself each time I resisted the urge to have a smoke. I was moving to something I wanted, rather than trying to eradicate a "flaw" in my character. This provided me with the necessary energy to quit. It was a shift from viewing myself negatively to taking a positive view. This is the only attitude you want to have about yourself when you're planning a change.

## The disaster and the miracle

Have you ever asked, "Who pulled the rug out from under me?" You're moving along and life is just the way you like it. Then a drastic change occurs—at least, it seems drastic to you at the time. Initially, it appears as if things never will get better; everything starts to look gray. In success stories, you seldom hear about these times. Storytellers neglect the lows; all you hear about is the highs. They forget to communicate how these down periods usually lead to the great successes, to positive shifts. In business, working with many successful people, I've learned that they all experience these highs and lows. When you're flat on your back, it helps to know that successful people have had these moments of despair and loss too.

You're not dysfunctional just because you have down-times; it's all part of a growth cycle. You grow, things are good, and then an event occurs that initially appears to be the *disaster* but, in the end, it stimulates you to further growth and self-expression. Really, it's a magnificent process! While the catastrophe is happening it's very hard to accept that anything can get better, but it does. The disaster can be emotional, or mental, or physical in nature. For Dave, the event involved all three aspects of himself.

⌒

A tow truck driver in his forties, Dave was directing traffic in the area of an accident. The driver of a car failed to follow the signs and Dave's direction. As a result, the car pinned Dave against a gravel truck, severing his leg. Later, in therapy, he recounted how suicidal he was. He was also furious with the driver. Excessive self-medication with alcohol did not help him control these negative feelings. Life was black for him; he was full of despair. Dave recounted that as he hit bottom he decided he had better make his life worth living. Today, Dave lives a full, financially successful life and has no problems with alcohol. He claims that without the disaster, he would not have achieved the rich and satisfying life he enjoys today.

⌒

Mike's story is slightly different. Mike was a highly successful CEO of a company he had made the favorite of investors. You can imagine his shock and amazement when his board of directors dismissed him. Over the next six months I watched Mike slowly digest this disaster. By the time a year had passed, he was well on his way to another successful corporate career. He took what was really a shell company, invested in it personally, and made it operational. Within two years Mike's success far outstripped his previous achievement as a CEO. Mike claims that if he hadn't experienced the dismissal, he would never know the success he now enjoys.

I use the word "miracle" in the title for this section because when the disaster strikes the final outcome is often too good to be believable. Neither Dave nor Mike would have believed the results of their change scenarios when the progression of events started. My life is very similar; when I look back, I see many events that I term miracles. There is no way I could have believed at the start of a particular disaster scenario that it would end the way it did.

It is difficult to find a joyous person who hasn't had what other people would call disasters or moments of despair. Yet, these misfortunes have provided an opportunity to tap previously unknown resources. When the disaster hits, there is that initial time that verges on hopelessness when you have to hang in there, knowing that change is inevitable. In two situations, people I have known took their own lives during this time of despair. In both instances, the challenge that caused them to give up hope had already been met. Unfortunately, they lacked the patience to wait for the good news that was on the way.

Remember, change is inevitable. Start listing the assets you do have at the moment. Before long you'll be provided an opportunity to use them. I am a firm believer the universe wastes none of its assets, which includes you. When you take control of your life and commit to the process of change, good things happen.

## Find your power

You can only change yourself; you can never change anyone else. Frequently, in my years of practice, parents wanted me to tell them how to change their children. Spouses came in asking for help to "change my husband" or "change my wife." These people were very disappointed when they learned that they could only change themselves. But when you pause and reflect for a moment, you see that this is really wonderful. It is ultimately liberating—if you cannot change anyone else, you cannot take responsibility for anyone else. If you acknowledge you can change only yourself, then you are in complete control.

*Control* is the keyword here, for how can you take responsibility for something you cannot direct? It would be insane. So relax—it is good news that you can change only you.

When it comes to relationships, though, there's an interesting side effect to your changes. A basic law of physics states that for every action, there is an opposite and equal reaction. What does this mean in terms of relationships? It means that when you change, most likely people you are involved with will also make a shift. Naturally their movement lags behind yours, and the shift may not be in the direction you wish. The steps they take are not in your control. Remember: having control means taking responsibility for others in your relationships. So to stay burden-free, all you have to do is keep focusing on the changes you want to achieve. Eventually, others either adapt or are no longer in a relationship with you.

At first glance this may seem rather brutal to you. In actual fact, it's loving and supportive of your significant others. You are saying you believe in them by allowing them to take responsibility for themselves. You are no longer trying to manipulate them by some strategy to get them to change their behavior. Putting it simply, everyone is granted the opportunity to take renewed control of their lives. Recovering alcoholics experience this process graphically. Most often, when their sobriety becomes a reality, the majority of their relationships change. The real meaning to all this is starkly simple: when you change, your life can no longer continue on its usual path. When you change, your world changes. What an empowering thought! But how do you tell the difference between what you feel you *should* do and what you actually *want* to change?

## Forget your shoulds: honor your wants

If you're like me, you were programmed with a lot of *shoulds* as you were growing up. The shoulds came from many different sources and sank pretty deeply into your consciousness. You probably received your shoulds in life before you were aware of your wants. I call *wants* those goals or desires that are prompting you to expand your life, to blossom like a flower. As a result, the shoulds often block or restrict your awareness of your wants, so your growth is restricted since your desires are ignored.

I was programmed to believe that wants were an expression of self-indulgence, and it was questionable whether I deserved having them fulfilled. My shoulds were pro-grammed as virtuous goals; they were self-sacrificing and I demonstrated strong character if I pursued them. Thank goodness life has helped me deprogram a lot of these ideas! I was in my late thirties before someone told me the mean-ing and source of the word "desire." It really means coming from the source—"de" meaning "of" and "sire" meaning "father" or "source." This insight helped me see that my wants or desires were really my inner urgings to express myself more fully. Shoulds originate from outside; they are external to you. Wants originate from within; they are part of the unique expression that is you.

If you have difficulty telling the difference between shoulds and wants, your body will provide assistance. When you think of a should, your body tenses up. You feel re-stricted, you're not relaxed, your energy level drops. You do not feel joyous or liberated. You feel there's something missing about you, something that is undone. You may even feel twinges of guilt. You also know that if you respond to the should, you'll still feel somewhat empty or frustrated.

Wants give you an entirely different feeling. Wants are like magnets; you are pulled to satisfy them. When you think of a want or desire, you can feel your energy level auto-matically rise. Your body responds; it becomes more mobile and flexible. Your mind starts generating ideas on how to fulfill your desires. It's like stepping out of confinement into the open countryside. You are all of a sudden much more alive. You feel expansive.

Watching clients' body language during therapy, I could immediately determine whether they were describing wants or shoulds. My challenge then was to help them differen-tiate between the two. This was important because of the low probability of a should being fulfilled by action. The opposite is true for wants, with which there is a high probability of fulfillment. My goal was for my clients to experience growth—meaning change and achievement. It was very important to me that they be working on wants, so they would take action, experience a shift, and achieve something different. To help them differentiate between shoulds and wants, I would often have them stand and say a should out loud. They would feel their knees lock and sense themselves leaning backwards slightly. A should is an external force, so naturally they would have to brace themselves and resist. Then, while they were still standing, I had them express a want. Their body would tend to move forward; sometimes they'd even take a little step to maintain their balance.

A want is something you are willing to move towards to fulfill. Even your body knows the difference. To experience this movement, try the first exercise and note your energy level rising and falling with the different wants and shoulds statements.

If it's really something you want to do, your body will become energized. You'll be motivated; you will want to get going. If you don't react positively, then the topic is

---

**Exercise:** *Clarifying wants and shoulds*

1. Start listening to the conversations you have with yourself—your self-talk. Choose a conversation, or monologue, in which you tell yourself you should do a particular thing. The should statement goes like this: "I should quit smoking."

2. Take the same topic and insert it into a want statement. The want statement is simply "I want to..."

probably a should, and you will be best to forget it. If it's a should, there is a low probability you will carry out the intent. Save your energy for something you truly want to do. You will be a much happier individual. The world will also benefit, because it will not have to live with a restrained and restricted you living out your shoulds.

## You have liftoff!

A certain amount of stability is required to make effective changes. You need a foundation to stand on while you make the changes you desire. Many things in life are quite functional, and they change at their own pace. Marriage is a good example. In most relationships a strong, healthy, constructive bond allows change to occur of its own accord. Both partners in these relationships change as they mature, as life matures them. They extend themselves automatically, and they allow their relationship to support this growth. With their partnership a constant in their lives, stability exists for both partners, enabling them to experience greater self-expansion.

The idea that you need a certain amount of stability in your life in order to make changes may sound paradoxical and contradictory. Here is an example that might help. Have you ever looked through binoculars on a rocking boat to see what direction you want to go? It would be much easier if you were standing on a rock. It's very difficult to figure out what is going on when everything is moving. You need a reasonably stable base and a foundation to build on in order to become a visionary or a progressive mover.

Effective change also requires some planning and preparation. Whenever there is a major undertaking, extensive planning and preparation are required to provide the necessary stability and support for the project. Whenever you're in the midst of change, and you feel planning and preparation are a waste of time, reflect for a moment on the level of support required for a space shuttle launch. When you're making changes in your life, you too are launching into new territory and breaking barriers. Allow yourself periods of time for planning and preparation.

Given the importance of some stability in your life and the need for preparation, it's no surprise then that changes you don't expect are the greatest challenge. Understanding how to use these events to your benefit provides you with the skills to thrive. The next chapter shows you how to shed energy-depleting encumbrances and focus your thrust on what you want. You are shown how to shift the negative reactions of fear, anger, guilt, and resistance to self-empowering actions, which positively affect all aspects of your life. You are lifted from discouraging uncertainty to a new level—to a valuing of life that you could never have envisioned before that unexpected event rocked your world.

Chapter 2

# Reversing Catastrophes

Events often bring change when we least expect it. Sometimes we have forewarning, other times no warning at all. Unexpected events may include being laid off or requested to retire early. Divorce or the death of a partner moves us from being part of a couple to living in the world of singles again. When these events occur without our wanting them to, we experience feelings and reactions that restrict our energy flow. When we deal with these feelings, the blocked energy can be released and redirected towards effecting beneficial change. I have seen many different reactions from clients and have used the following helpful techniques to assist them through unexpected situations.

## Boost your energy: release denial and resistance

Have you ever resisted acknowledging what is happening right before your eyes? Your denial makes it difficult for you to handle change. The simple act of resistance depletes energy, even if you are not consciously aware that you are resisting.

To experience the energy needed to resist, have someone stand behind you and place their hands on your shoulders. Have them gently push ahead while you resist stepping forward. The energy used for this physical resistance will be apparent to you. It is very similar to the energy required emotionally and mentally to deny conditions in your life.

Within the body, resistance causes a negative kind of stress. It is the kind of stress that lowers the immune system's ability to handle disease. In fact, we live in a state of "dis-ease" when we resist. When we allow and acknowledge existing conditions, immediately we begin to feel more relaxed and able to cope. Soon we realize that we are more effective. We become aware of new and different solutions to our change challenge.

The act of denial extracts another price from us. When we deny a situation, we delay attending to it. This robs us of the joy and satisfaction that come from dealing with situations as they arise. Acknowledging a situation early in the process does not mean we will necessarily act immediately to change it. We may decide to defer taking action. The act of making a conscious decision, though, allows the release of energy that would previously be consumed by resistance or denial. Conscious action—despite the fact that we are often fearful of acting—is an energizing event. It gives us self-confidence and empowers us. It is one way to move out of the victim state.

## Save yourself from victim prison

All of us feel we have been victimized at one time or another. We feel that events beyond our control have occurred, and we have ended up on the short end of the stick. We feel external forces are in control. "They" did it to us.

Because we feel disempowered, we look for someone else to solve our problem. We look to the source of our victimization or to some third party to rectify it. We may even beseech God to cure it. We don't feel we have the power or the control to accomplish the necessary changes ourselves. Usually this "makes" us angry, and often we experience some grieving. But the end result is we feel that we were taken advantage of and we feel powerless. Releasing the feeling of victimization is essential to positive change and growth. If we feel "done to," we do not own our power. We must reclaim our power to move on.

Several steps are helpful in releasing those negative feelings. The first step is to realize we have chosen the victim stance. I was about eleven years old, living on a small farm in rural Canada, when my parents separated. Being the only capable boy at home, I was left with a fair number of farm chores. One night, one of my friends stayed with me. Together, we fed the cows and horses and did other farm chores that his dad did on their farm. He suggested that I was being hard-done-by, that the chores were a man's work. I denied it at the time. But I mulled it over and, by the end of the month, I agreed with him—I was definitely a victim. Life was grossly unfair. I decided that I was being treated poorly. It was years before I dealt with those feelings. The first step to change was realizing that *I decided* whether I was a victim or not. I decided whether the unexpected event that altered my life was beneficial, detrimental, or neutral.

Accepting that we have made this decision frees us to realize that we can un-make it. We are accountable only to ourselves in this regard; if we want to feel victimized, we can. But by the same token, if we want to liberate ourselves from that state and feel more empowered, we can do that, too. We have that freedom. All we have to do is decide that we are not being victimized, that the situation we are in *just is*. We can choose to see that it has nothing to do with us personally, other than offering a learning experience. I came to understand that my father's leaving had nothing to do with me. I just happened to be there—a neutral agent.

The second step in overcoming victimization is to look at the event and see what good can come out of it. I was in my late thirties before I realized my parents' separation helped me develop independence and added to my coping skills. It was a truly beneficial experience for me, and I acquired some real, positive spin-off. That realization allowed me to overcome the feeling of being a victim and release my anger towards my parents. When I stopped being a victim, I could make that big change.

Suppose you have been employed for ten years but have now been terminated because of downsizing. To free yourself from the victim trap, it helps to consider what those ten years have given you. What skills have you learned that you can transfer to a new job? What friendships and networks were you able to develop? Begin to view your situation within the context of the benefits you have gained. You may see that downsizing grants you the freedom to more fully utilize the skills you learned during your employment.

The final step is to decide what action to take because now you are ready to move on. Why not let go? Why not release the feeling of being victimized? Look at it as a turning point—an event that has great potential to contribute to your growth.

## Free yourself from fear

Your resistance to change is always linked to fear. Fear comes a close second to love in running your life. Where love expands and motivates you to grow, fear prompts you to behave in many destructive ways. Hate is often said to be the opposite of love, but if you look behind hate, you will find the prompter—fear. All our controlling, destructive behavior stems from fear. This is so frequently demonstrated in personal relationships. It is fear that causes one partner to attempt to control the other, who in turn responds with a fear reaction. In many relationships, this fear builds until it becomes strong enough to restrict vulnerability and stifle intimacy. For some, the scenario continues until the relationship is dead.

In work relationships, again fear is a destructive element. So often the employer, because of fear, attempts to take advantage of employees. Similarly, the employees respond to this fear with the formation of unions, work-to-rule, and other strategies. As a result, both parties are frustrated in achieving their goals. To manage change, we have to accept responsibility for our fear. If we don't, our problems increase. When we blame others or external conditions for our fearful state, we feel further disempowered. We end up handing over control of our lives to the object of our fear. Unless we address it, fear creates fear and eventually controls us.

When I was six years old living on the farm, I often visited a neighbor lady who loved me as my mother did. On one occasion, night was falling as I started out by myself to walk the mile home. The route was through the woods; there were no lights but a good path. I was over halfway home when I heard footsteps behind me. In no time at all, I imagined that half of the predators in the animal kingdom were about to attack me. I pictured a coyote, then a wolf, then a bear.

I started running to escape but before long I was out of breath, with no alternative but to stop and hope that the beast wasn't hungry and simply wanted to play. I still remember sitting down by the path preparing myself for the inevitable. Of course, as soon as I stopped, the footsteps stopped also. I soon realized my predator was my fear.

Facing and accepting your fear, while scary, is a freeing experience. Even if there really is a "beast," you can deal with it much more effectively by facing it. Denial only increases your fear. As your fear mounts, you become more inflexible, making change difficult, sometimes impossible. It is much easier to examine your fears—to determine what is real and

### Exercise: *Using your fear*

1. With a pen and a pad of paper, sit quietly for five to ten minutes.
2. Write down the fear you are feeling.
3. Write down the worst situation that could result if you took action in response to your fear. Suppose you fear your child is using illegal drugs, and the action you are considering is confrontation. Possibly, the worst situation is to discover your child is indeed using drugs; your fear is confirmed.
4. Examine this worst-case scenario and determine how you would deal with it and survive its passing. Using the same example, you would probably try to determine how serious your child's drug usage is. Based on the findings, you would most likely seek appropriate help for your child.
5. Now envision the next most negative event that might occur if you acted to resolve the fearful situation. Then envision how you would deal with it. Write down both your imaginings. Using our example, possibly the next worst reaction would be for the child to deny the usage and be hurt by

what is imaginary—than to wait for mental or physical collapse. When you deal with the problem in this constructive manner, you experience liberation. Your fears seldom vanish completely, but you can learn to live with them, manage them, and use them to motivate you. When you own your fears and take responsibility for them, you are then motivated to take action. In actuality, your fears can assist you in accomplishing what you desire.

When you stand up and look your fear in the eye, you are starting to deal with it. You can develop alternatives to what you are doing right now and start making positive changes in your life. The exercise "Using your fear" demontrates how your fear can move you to action.

Judy, an accountant and single mother in her mid-thirties, learned to use fear to accomplish changes in her life.

your accusation. You would probably respond by telling your child your concern is coming from love and your desire to be protective.

6. Write down the probability of the two situations occurring.

7. Examine the current situation that is prompting your fear. Ask yourself, "Will it get worse or better if I don't take any action?"

8. If your answer is that it's liable to get worse, then now is the time to act. You have already confirmed to yourself that you can handle the worst-case scenarios. You've also found, I suspect, that the probability that the worst will happen is less than fifty percent. It's a situation gamblers love—the odds are with you.

9. If you believe that by not acting your current situation is going to get better, then the appropriate "action" is to be patient and allow the situation to improve with time. By practising this exercise, you will discover a course of action. A shift or change has occurred; fear no longer immobilizes you. You are now using fear to your advantage.

She abused alcohol and had recently been found guilty of assault. Judy was sent by the courts to see me. During our first session, it was evident that Judy's habitual way of dealing with fear was to get angry and to intimidate others. This gave her control and reduced her fear level but did not provide a satisfactory solution. Now she was faced with a court order, which threatened her personal freedom. She was determined to see the people she wanted to see, when she wanted to see them, free of control by the court. I was certainly not a person she wanted to see. Her anger was so intense that our first session was going nowhere; then I asked her how she dealt with her fear. Judy denied that she had any fear. She further described how she had controlled all the men in her life, how she had stood up to anyone representing authority. In her words, she was fearless. It was only when we explored this need for control that Judy realized, yes, she was very fearful.

Over the next several sessions, Judy learned to use her fear constructively. Whatever situation she feared, she investigated and attempted positive action. For instance, she used her fear of authority to deal with her probation officer. Instead of acting belligerently, Judy decided to make an attempt to talk with him. She would find out about the difficulties of his job and treat him as a person instead of the "monster" she described. The officer responded positively to Judy's new approach.

By moving from denying to accepting her fear, she found ways of getting more cooperation and fewer restrictions from the court. Over the course of months, she was reunited with her family and found it possible to live without self-medicating with alcohol. All these changes were possible when she accepted her fear. She was able to literally sit down with her fear and use it to motivate herself to positive action.

My clients and my personal experiences have taught me that we always have the capacity to cope with the source of our fears. The beauty is that we grow every time we deal with our fear. We gain the sense of greater competency and joy, allowing us to deal with challenges that have plagued us for many years.

## Mine the energy of anger

Anger can be helpful in achieving change, although it does have its limitations and must be used cautiously. It energizes you and allows you to take action. Let's examine anger to understand how this happens.

Anger is a reaction to fear—not an emotion but purely a reaction, a gift, to help you deal with fear. As you start getting angry, adrenaline is released into your system, and many other physical changes occur. Less blood circulates and less oxygen reaches your brain, restricting your ability to think rationally. This in turn allows you to focus totally on the problem in a knee-jerk reaction, but it does not guarantee rational action. As your anger builds, your ability to act rationally decreases sharply to the point at which anger controls you. We all know the term "blind rage," which is what occurs if you let your anger go unchecked. At this point, it does not serve you.

So, in the initial stages, anger can be used constructively. You maintain control and use anger only to energize or motivate yourself to take action. You can use it to deal with the situation that is confronting you. Often anger is the push that propels you forward.

Once the anger reaction starts, it is not healthy to ignore it. Either deal with the situation or release the anger. If left unattended, it sits and builds, becoming a bomb ready to explode. Several years ago, I experienced this personally. I was meeting with my staff at a retreat on corporate planning. The meeting had begun early in the morning. At lunch break, I realized that I was becoming frustrated with two managers who I felt were busy building their own empires. I believed they were doing this rather than attending to the health of the whole company. I was angry at this competition but did not act.

My anger continued to build throughout the day. After dinner in another meeting session, I exploded with a verbal diatribe that didn't make sense even to me. When I regained control, I realized what had happened. If I had dealt with my anger early in the day, the whole tone of the meeting and the results achieved would probably have been quite different. For me, it was a definitive learning experience on anger management.

Anger can be easily misused. The accompanying adrenaline rush gives you a sense of power. Using anger to generate this sense of power can be habit-forming. It is very easy to slip into the pattern and use anger to get attention. You want others to change, and you use your anger in an attempt to control them. You blame others for your anger and expect them to respond in the way you desire. "You made me angry" is a caution flag when you say it either out loud or in your self-talk.

As soon as we become aware that we are blaming others for our anger, it's time to look at what's going on. It is very important that we own our anger and take responsibility for it—otherwise, we cannot control it. By blaming others for our anger, we are granting them control over us. Our feelings of powerlessness magnify, we are threatened with greater fear, and even more anger results. At this point, outside professional help can be a benefit. The purpose of a therapist is to provide feedback, for often we are unaware of how frequently we are getting angry and giving control over ourselves to others.

Facilitating anger management groups demonstrated to me how this whole anger process works. Many of the participants had been ordered by the court to attend the group. Despite the threat hanging over their heads—attend the sessions or serve time in jail—they had difficulty accepting responsibility for their anger. It was impossible for them to make changes while blaming others for their predicament. Once the process of accepting responsibility for their anger began, changes followed. Taking responsibility gave them control of their anger, which led to a feeling of empowerment that facilitated other changes in their lives.

Kurt was one angry person who made startling changes in his life. He had been in trouble with the law since his early teens. Now twenty-seven, he had done jail time on many occasions. During our initial one-to-one meeting, Kurt felt he was being forced to attend the group sessions. Because he did not like either alternative, he could not see that "jail or group" gave him any choice at all. Finally, he accepted that he had freedom of choice in the matter and the responsibility to choose. This was a beginning for Kurt. He started examining where his anger was directed and what responsibility he had in response to his anger. He realized he could act to resolve past frustrations. In the end, his anger energized him to deal with numerous past conflicts and to heal old wounds.

Kurt was typical of many people in the groups. The key was to accept responsibility for their anger, which led to a feeling of freedom and choice, which in turn was empowering. Properly utilized anger contributes significantly to a better life. The energy derived from anger can be effectively directed to make the changes we desire.

## Let go of your anxiety

Anxiety, really, is an expression of fear. Anxiety has many levels from mild to severe, with accompanying physical effects. If you allow your anxiety to go uncontrolled for long, you'll probably experience anxiety attacks. You suffer shortness of breath, sometimes dizziness, nausea, and in acute cases, fainting. Physically, the problem is lack of oxygen to the brain. Your body goes into a fear response to equip you to deal with danger. Since the danger does not exist—it's actually in the future—the body cannot get relief by physically responding to the danger. Instead, it maintains

**Exercise:** *Clarifying anxiety*

Have someone you trust and who supports your growth ask you these questions:
- What concerns do you have for the future?
- Are these concerns within your control?
- What action can you take today to reduce your anxiety?
- What feelings do you have when you take control of your worries?

When you understand the source of your anxiety and can see how to change it, you become relaxed, joyous, and solution-focused.

a high state of alert preparedness. Eventually, in severe cases, the body takes over and you faint. If you are in good physical health, you resume consciousness and return to breathing normally. Your brain starts receiving its normal supply of oxygen, and your anxiety attack symptoms disappear for the time being.

The source of anxiety lies with some fear in the future, a time space that you cannot deal with because you're not there yet. You are and can only be in the present moment. You are actually dealing with situations you describe as "What if?" Often you are not aware of the fear that produces your anxiety, and it is helpful for someone to question you about your "worries." This person is someone you trust and who is free of any need to be responsible for you. Ideally, this person is a coach or trusted friend. Once you have selected this trusted person, do the exercise "Clarifying anxiety."

Rationally, you can approach the anxiety by realizing its source does not exist yet. It lies in the future and when it comes into existence, you will deal with it as you have many other challenges. You will handle it as best you can and continue as you have in the past.

**Exercise:** *Handling anxiety*

- Pick an object near you and focus on it. Examine it closely and hear yourself describing it to someone else.
- Involve yourself in a physical activity—walking, running, yoga, stretching.
- Take deep breaths. Breathe deeply and count. In one, two, three. Out one, two, three. Take up to ten deep breaths. Anchor the deep breathing to another activity that you do throughout the day such as going to the bathroom.

Emotionally, the key to letting go of anxiety is to retrieve your focus from the future to the present. Three methods for doing that are outlined in the exercise "Handling anxiety" on page 31.

If you are experiencing anxiety attacks, the simple breathing exercise oxygenates the body through the day. Periods of relaxation follow. You pause and relax, look around and start living in the present moment. You find yourself coping, and that fact alone is empowering. It quells fear and stops the vicious cycle of anxiety building on anxiety.

With decreased anxiety levels, you can take many other emotional and physical steps to gain greater peace and calmness. Meditation and rhythmic physical exercise are very helpful. They both bring you into the present moment and help you become aware that often you are thinking and living in the future.

I find myself becoming anxious when I ask myself questions that I can't know the answer to for another ten or fifteen years. How will it feel when I retire? What will I do? I can take steps to prepare myself for retirement, but I can't answer all the questions. I don't know how I will feel—I'm not there yet. And that's true for us all. How will you meet your death? How will you handle it? You can prepare for it, but you're not there yet.

Working with seniors, I've found that often it isn't the fear of death that is a worry, but how they will die. And death is like all change. It helps if you make some preparations or have a vision of what you want. You can plan your death to some extent; you can plan who you would like to have around as the time draws near. Some questions to ask are:

- How would I like to deal with my estate?
- What kind of memorial or funeral service would I prefer?
- What is my favorite music?
- Who would I want to deliver my eulogy? Why not ask that person while I'm alive?

You can make some preparations and calm yourself that way. When you're dealing with the future, you can often take some action now. The action will not completely resolve the problem, and there's no guarantee your plans will be followed, but it reduces your anxiety now. Anxiety, worry, and stress stem from your feeling of powerlessness—that you are helpless to deal with a certain situation. So help yourself by creating a desired vision that deals with future anxiety-ridden situations. Long-term relief will only come when you change your beliefs about yourself and the world around you. When this happens your self-talk, or brain chatter, becomes positive and free of anxiety.

## Transcend worry

*Worry is like a rocking chair. It gives you something to do but doesn't get you anywhere.*    Author Unknown

Good friends gave me this simple homily written on a little wooden plaque. Why would they do that? I am a man of varied experiences, one who has known success and failure and learned from both. My friends gave me the gift because worry creeps up on most, if not all, of us. It sneaks into our minds as a minor troubling thought, not enough to "worry" about. Soon, through repetitive self-talk, we have prodded ourselves into a full-blown snit. Many of us play out dramas in our minds and envision scenarios that would make a science fiction writer envious.

Worry is a domain that first teases us but eventually possesses us, with the resulting loss of joy. From a change perspective, worry leads to inaction, and we become procrastinators. This is the very opposite of what many of us believe. We think if we want to change a situation we need to "take it seriously." This is another way of saying "worry about it." Supposedly, the idea is that when we worry, we are in pursuit of solutions, but it is erroneous to believe that we can find an answer by concentrating on the problem. We know that what we focus on grows. We attract more of the same. So worrying about a solution to a challenge moves us further away from the actual solution and only creates more worries.

When your mind keeps finding its way back to worrying, try the exercise "Minimizing worry." Performing this exercise prevents worry from draining your energy during the day. It also significantly decreases the number of

**Exercise:** *Minimizing worry*

1. Consciously set aside a specific time in your day and a definite amount of time to worry—fifteen minutes maximum. At that time, you will put all of your energy and focus into worrying. During the day, whenever you are aware of a worry, write it down on a piece of paper. Then, at the designated time, address all these written concerns for the fifteen minutes.

2. It helps to have an object to handle or fondle during your worry session. Worry beads or small pebbles work well. Fingering these objects helps you focus on the worry and affords the satisfaction of giving your worries the attention they deserve.

3. Make certain that you observe the fifteen-minute time limit. If you don't finish, save the topics for the next session.

worries you create. I use the word "create" deliberately, because you do have a choice here. You absolutely don't need to worry; it does not lead to successful living.

You can be certain, though, that whether you use deliberate action to stop worrying or you continue to worry, your worries will eventually cease. Intense and serious worrying leads to a breakdown of your physical health. You are shut down, forced to stop worrying because you are no longer physically capable of this activity. I experienced this graphically several years ago.

Our community was going through a major economic readjustment; some people called it a recession. As a consultant, I felt vulnerable; I felt that work was precarious. I had been working diligently on creating a small oil company, and I had been told that I would head the company. Then one morning I received the news it was not going to happen. That night I was admitted to hospital with a blood clot in my lung. I lay there reflecting, asking myself, "What am I doing here? What's going on? What's my body trying to

---

**Exercise:** *Transcending your concerns*

Do this exercise without focusing on how the solution will be carried out. Let your imagination and freethinking soar.

1. Write down your most serious concern.

2. Imagine a genie able to grant whatever you desire.

3. Ask the genie for a solution to your challenge. Write it down.

4. Organize the solution into steps.

5. List the steps in the order you must complete them.

6. Break down the first step into a small enough increment that you can comfortably work on it right now, today.

tell me?" I realized it was telling me to stop worrying, that worry was not going to produce a helpful solution. I had become like a hamster in a cage, running until I'd almost exhausted myself. But, before that happened, my body said whoa! With a blood clot in my lung, I had to stop worrying in order to recover my health.

When I reflect on this situation, I appreciate what a wonderful creation we are. Imagine a built-in system that gently prods us with symptoms of stress—tension in our bodies, headaches—telling us change is needed. When we ignore the gentle prods, we eventually get the "hammer." We are forced to stop in our path and cease our stress-producing worrying. Then finally our focus shifts from problems and fear to solutions and strength. I have learned that when we get locked into worry, it is very difficult to see a possible solution. The exercise "Transcending your concerns" on page 35 assists in creating solutions to your worries.

As you visualize the solution, a feeling of relief comes from the release of your worries. At this point, you have a plan that you can work with to solve your challenge. Often you will find that the intermediate steps lead you to a different final step or solution than you originally imagined. This is natural, as you have now reframed your challenge to actually looking for solutions. You have a much greater chance of overcoming your concern when you focus on a solution rather than the problem.

Here is a simpler process. Every time you become aware you are worrying, write down a possible solution. When my clients acted on this suggestion between sessions, they almost always reported miraculous results. We all have tremendous capabilities and insights on how to handle life challenges. Our real problem is not the problem itself, but our ability to shift our mental and emotional focus to finding the solution.

## Attention! Attention! You have stress

Many illnesses are caused when our bodies say it's time to change our behavior. My experience with cancer suggests just that. I was on a real guilt trip over my failed marriage, and my body said, Hey—you need to examine what's going on. I felt my body was asking, Is this guilt functional? My feelings of guilt had weakened my immune system; this I believe triggered the cancer. I'm not suggesting that cancer manifests because we design it or anything like that. What I am suggesting is that our body uses many signals to warn us that the route we're currently traveling or the way we are behaving needs to shift to restore health to our total organism—our emotions, mind, body. When we're not functioning in harmony, one part of this organism will signal the other parts that change is required. Often the body acts out the signal. Whenever I experience an illness, I examine what the signal is about. What's the warning? What's showing on my organism radar screen? This total organism that I call myself is dedicated to my welfare, to my living in harmony.

## Glean the gifts in depression

If, during times of depression, you were to observe your behaviors on an oscilloscope, the peaks on the screen would flatten out. You become quieter. You move more slowly. But, despite the blue feelings, periods of depression can be constructive. They become an excellent time for reflection. Depression has the potential to be a gestation period for creativity. Seizing this opportunity, you will find the depression is nothing to be depressed about. I can understand if your initial reaction to this statement is frustration. I felt that way when an understanding coach once said to me, "Hugh, have a good depression." Upon reflection, I realized he was not being flippant but was quite sincere. He meant that the depression was a time for me to examine what was going on in my life, to see where I would like to make a change. Oddly enough, when I started using depression creatively, I was left with two positive results. First, I was no longer depressed and, second, I had a plan for the future. Ultimately, this means you and I no longer have to waste times of depression but can use them creatively.

You may feel that this won't work for long periods of acute depression. While this is a book about change, and not about depression, let me offer these thoughts. As a rule when you are depressed, you experience low levels of energy and thus avoid activity. In many ways you are immobilized and have, in a sense, opted out of life. When you say, "It's hopeless," you are acting in a similar fashion to people who have anxiety. Life is hopeless because your focus is on trying to solve some past or future problem. This is indeed hopeless, because you cannot live in those time spaces. When you refocus to the present, the depression lifts and remains lifted as long as you are focused in the moment—a difficult task for those living in the future-oriented western world. In the present, you can have impact on your world. You can take action and make positive changes in your life. The process is really the same regardless of whether the depression is slight or severe.

Naturally, all this is easier said than done. When you are depressed, it's difficult to summon enough energy to act.

Often it's a great gift if someone asks for your help. By responding to their request for assistance you become re-energized; you start the energy flowing. You also find a sense of worth. If you are in a depressed state, consider performing a service for someone else. You will be the beneficiary. It's a good example of how our lives are entwined; when you help someone else, it does wonders for your sense of being. It's like the sun coming out after a rain shower. Everything is alive, sparkling clean, and vibrant. Life becomes a joy.

While you are depressed, it's difficult to create a shift in your life. Yet the fact that you are depressed suggests that you need to make changes. So the next time you're feeling low, rather than heaping self-criticism and a lot of other smelly stuff on yourself, think of it as a time for creativity. Fill yourself with thoughts of how you would like to change your life. It may be time to re-create a vision for yourself. Use your next low period as a springboard for change. How to do this is explained in the following chapter.

## Say goodbye to guilt

Expansive, productive growth does not come out of guilt. Guilt produces the opposite. When we feel guilty our shoulders slump, and we restrict our vision downward. Using a "dog" metaphor, we put our tail between our legs and run. We become apologetic and retreat.

Others commonly use guilt to control us and to motivate us to change. Yet, it is not effective. All it does is render us less capable of making the desired change.

In my marriage counseling work, I found partners using guilt frequently. "You don't want to make love anymore," states the husband. His wife replies, "Well, you're a rotten lover." It is possible that both these statements are true, but they are certainly not constructive; they are designed to produce guilt.

The situation improves dramatically when the statements are altered: "I find you so attractive that I want to make love more often." The attractive part must be true or why would he want to make love to her? Her reply is a turn-on for many a male ego: "I'd like to change some of our love-making habits—are you up to the challenge?" No one is being put down in this last exchange; there is an invitation for change but not a demand. Remember, earlier we stated that we couldn't change anyone else.

When we attack through guilt, we encourage the other person to go on the defensive and firmly entrench themselves in their position. They also are prone to attack us with guilt accusations, making the situation even more difficult for positive change.

Guilt is interwoven with our society. We don't realize it, but frequently we attack ourselves with self-talk that is comprised of guilt statements. "I should be more loving," or "I should be more forgiving." What is a should statement really saying about us? It says we are somehow inadequate. There is an implication that we *should* feel guilty.

Removing guilt releases large amounts of energy back into our everyday lives so we can be freer and live with greater joy. We can also learn techniques to avoid feeling guilty. First, when we are told we are wrong, regardless of the source, we can regard it only as a stop sign—a request that we stop our present behavior—not as an indication that we have a personality or character flaw. These statements are a commentary on our behavior only, not on our person.

Often we need to reframe a guilt statement, from an

absolute truth about us to one about our behavior. It is not that we are bad people, but that our behavior needs changing. Changing behavior is far easier than changing who we feel we are and what we represent. People feeling guilty over crimes they've committed need to go through this process before they can be rehabilitated. As long as we feel our person is being condemned, we feel disempowered and victimized. Positive changes under these conditions are difficult, if not impossible. I was made very much aware of this when I worked with people convicted of crimes. Being remorseful over their inappropriate behavior was constructive, but feeling that society viewed them as flawed people was not. If they could not believe in their own worth and capability, they were unable to change their behavior. Peter was an excellent example of this dynamic.

A university student, Peter was twenty-two years old when his girlfriend died as a result of his driving drunk. He was sent to prison for manslaughter and came to me during his subsequent parole period. He was overwhelmed by his guilt and incapable of making positive changes. Like a trapped animal, all he could do was lash out in anger, which made his rehabilitation even more difficult. He was angry with his parents for raising him in a home where alcohol was abused. He felt his parole conditions were a constant reminder that he was an inferior person and a menace to society. His guilt was so great he could not bear to meet with his deceased girlfriend's family.

After a few counseling sessions, Peter realized that it was his behavior and not his person that needed changing. He was then able to release his guilt, take responsibility for what he had done, and feel remorse for his actions. As a result, his anger and victim stance shifted. His newfound sense of worth enabled him to see he had something to offer his girlfriend's family. His meetings with them and their sharing of common grief greatly contributed to everyone's healing.

All this has taught me that guilt in its many forms and intensities does not produce constructive change. Guilt weakens us, we feel flawed and, therefore, less able to make change. When we can shift from condemning our own

---

**Exercise:** *Shedding guilt*

1. Take a pen and a notepad. (I like using pen and paper because it causes you to focus and slow down your thinking.) Write down the behavior that has resulted in your present guilt feelings. For example, you and your partner have an agreement to jointly discuss any purchases over $500. You have broken your word by buying a suit for $700—with no discussion. You feel guilty and have avoided telling your partner for the last three days.

2. Knowing the consequences of that behavior, how would you change your reaction in a similar scenario? Write down the troublesome situation and your new reaction to it. Using our example, you realize your guilt is not allowing you to enjoy the suit and has created a barrier between you and your partner. Your new reaction

might be: "Anytime I break my word, I will deal with it immediately and will not live the accompanying bad feelings."

3. Spend a moment or two reading and rereading what you have just written down. Does it fit for you? If not, change your reaction until you're comfortable with how you handle the situation.

4. Say out loud to yourself, "I now value myself to the extent that when (your guilt scenario) occurs, I will (your new reaction or behavior)." Repeat this commitment whenever you feel guilty about how you have behaved in the past. Returning to the example of the suit, your affirmation could be: "I am a strong person. I value myself to the extent I will take corrective action to deal with negative feelings as soon as possible."

person and see that it's only our behavior we need to change, we are able to start forgiving. When this happens, real change occurs.

Guilt and our sense of self-worth are very much connected. In Chapter 5, the discussion on self-worth will help deal with guilt. In the meantime, try the simple exercise "Shedding guilt."

Doing this exercise not only releases you from guilt but helps you learn from your past. You are able to see past regrettable behaviors not as mistakes, but as learning situations. That is truly what they are, and when you make that shift, your growth is greatly accelerated.

## Forgiveness: a key to health and wholeness

Forgiveness is the process of releasing the idea of revenge. We detach ourselves from the need to "get even" with the person who we perceive has wronged us. Now, forgiveness is very difficult when we feel we're doing it for the other person. We already feel they are somewhat unworthy. They deserve our anger, our hatred, our ill will. The question is, though, do we deserve to live in a state of anger and hatred and suffer the consequences? I personally think not. It doesn't help anyone, particularly ourselves. The amusing thing is that our anger links us to the person we are angry with. And the angrier we become, the stronger the bond. The most effective way of changing our anger is to look at the benefits of forgiveness. When we forgive and let go, all the energy that is tied up in anger and revenge-seeking becomes available for us to use constructively.

Suddenly, we're able to release that person or situation and to form a more constructive relationship. When we persist in holding on, we're being restricted. We're caged like an animal with the resentment we feel. It's ironic and paradoxical that we are literally and metaphorically handcuffed to the objects of our anger, despite this really being the last thing that we want. But when we forgive, the doors of the cage open and we're liberated.

Many of us were raised with the idea that forgiveness makes us a better person and frees the other person from our anger. This may be true but, actually, we are the main benefactors. We are no longer trapped in a victim's prison seeking revenge, or holding others ransom until they offer an apology. We are free to accept the change, to grow and build on the new life that change has created.

You would think this potential of joy would be enough to bring us to forgiveness. However, for many of us, it isn't. Despite the obvious, we still find it difficult to accept this point of view and release our anger. This stems from our years of practice in holding grudges. We have received immense payoffs for presenting ourselves as victims. To let go launches us into unfamiliar territory. We cling to the belief that we are right and they are wrong. To forgive them somehow would make them our equals, and they don't

---

**Exercise:** *Practising forgiveness*

1. Choose a mental image of someone you love and send them loving thoughts.
2. Now picture in your mind the person you want to "fix."
3. Try to send loving thoughts to that person and, as soon as you feel your anger, switch back to step 1.
4. Re-establish feelings of love, switch back to step 2, and then repeat step 3.
5. Do this for a maximum of five minutes. Return to the exercise later in the day or the next day.

deserve this status. They are wrong and thus deserve our anger. We feel it our duty to "fix" them, to set things right. Another pitfall is that we feel we deserve the right to be angry. But we also all have the right to joy, and we cannot have both at the same time. So which do you prefer, anger or joy?

It is the same for love. Seeking revenge and being angry with someone restricts our capacity for love. An exercise that demonstrates the exclusivity of love and revenge-seeking is "Practising forgiveness."

Eventually, you will find that by repeating this exercise you'll forgive the person or the persons you are angry with. It helps to remember you are only working on forgiving and not forgetting. No one expects you to forget what triggered the need to forgive. Instead, forgiveness is letting go of the sting and the need to get back at that person. Consider marriage relationships in which one member has broken commitment to the other. The offended partners need to forgive, but not necessarily forget, the broken commitment. Similarly, the offending partners must forgive themselves, so the relationships can become once more loving partnerships. When I worked with couples, I witnessed when forgiveness occurred and when it didn't. When forgiveness didn't happen (even when the couples stayed together) the relationship was filled with acrimony. When forgiveness occurred (even though the offending events were not necessarily forgotten) the relationship blossomed anew.

It is a paradox. Forgiveness itself is a shift, which needs to happen before we can take on other challenges. Forgiveness is necessary for our health and growth, so let us become conscious of what we are doing. We can grow by releasing our anger and stepping forward into the joy of being alive.

This moves us along the road to giving thanks for our life and all its experiences.

## Give thanks for your experience

Have you ever heard someone say, "That experience was the best thing that ever happened to me"? They may continue with, "At the time, though, I sure didn't think so." What they're saying is that there was an event in their life they initially felt was extremely negative. Something happened to them that they hadn't planned on, and at the time they regretted it. The event made a substantial impact on their lives. It put them on a different path and, eventually, they found that path rewarding—so rewarding that later they were thankful it happened.

I remember talking to a gentleman in his eighties who had an illustrious career as an author and speaker. Yet, in his early teens his plan was to be a concert violinist. When he was fourteen, someone stole his violin and dashed his hopes. He told me that at the time he was devastated and beyond consoling. It wasn't until after he completed university that he realized the theft of his violin was a blessing. He felt being a violinist would never have given him the satisfaction of what he was gaining now.

Another way of looking at unwanted events is to ask, "Would I trade my life for someone else's?" I am not talking about a person's possessions, lifestyle, or exterior trappings. I am referring to who they are and who they have become as a result of their experiences. I have yet to meet one person who would trade personalities. Perhaps people would trade life situations, but definitely not who they are. To a significant degree, your past life experiences have made you who you are. (I am not talking about past lives or reincarnation). Whether you judged the events good or bad, they all had an impact on you and contributed to who you have become. So, if you are in the midst of what you perceive as a calamity, hang in there! This calamity may be one of your most life-enriching events. Certainly, how you react to it and incorporate it in your life will be factors in who you become. You have some choices in how you react:

- You can react with bitterness and feel life has dealt you an unfair blow.
- You can deny the event happened and use a lot of energy in blocking out reality.
- You can acknowledge the event and take a wait-and-see attitude, perhaps even display curiosity about what will unfold as a result.
- You can become an active participant in your life.

There are other possible alternatives; however, of the four given here, it's obvious the last alternative will provide you the most joy.

Despite how apparent the most effective choice is, many of us spend considerable time after the event choosing the first or second alternative. If you are one of these people, be generous and forgiving with yourself. There is lots of outside support for those positions. What you do have to avoid is making a habit of choosing the first two alternatives. Become more aware that how you react is your choice. Become curious about life, always asking, "How can I handle this; what are my alternatives?" It also helps if you allow yourself to be aware you are handling it right now, and that is all you have to do at the present moment. You do not have to deal with tomorrow, because you are not there yet. And tomorrow—who knows—you may have a new set of circumstances and the means to deal differently with the event.

As you can see, your reaction to an event has a lot to do with change. Your reaction determines many subsequent events. It also has a lot to do with whether you experience joy or hardship in your life. Eventually, if you can look back at the event and be grateful for it, you will know you have entered a new era. I am not saying that you wish a similar event to reoccur, or that you're glad it happened. What I am saying is that you have become thankful for what the event caused or created in your life. You have moved beyond regretting the past and have realized that life means change and, without change, there is only stagnation and death. You accept that life-changing events are opportunities— opportunities for you to decide how you will react, opportunities for new, enriching experiences. Life cannot improve without change. Let's welcome life.

Once you welcome life, you really do become an active participant. Rather than feeling life is "doing it" to you, you become proactive. Part of being proactive is to draw a vision for your life. The next chapter helps you recall all your forgotten and varied dreams and desires. Use these aspirations to build a vision, which becomes the blueprint for all aspects of your life.

# Chapter 3

# Deciding the Dance:
# Your Vision (*Step One*)

This chapter holds the key to your becoming a change-master. If you do nothing else but complete the exercises in this chapter, you will receive returns many times the price you paid for this book. If I had only one suggestion to make, it would be "Create a vision for yourself!"

Have you ever felt you were drifting aimlessly and life was passing you by? Those are the symptoms of lacking a vision or being unaware of your vision for yourself. Imagine trying to travel to a destination when you don't know where it is, and you have no charts or maps to guide you on your way. Living without a vision of how you want to conduct your life and what you want to accomplish is equally impossible. Without a vision, it is dangerous to try to take control of your life. It is like sitting behind the steering wheel of a moving car with no idea where you want to steer it, a scenario that is bound to end in disaster. Without a vision, it is virtually impossible for you to handle change in a way that satisfies you.

## Look at the big picture

Everyone has an image of themselves. Do you like yours? Have you ever thought of changing your self-image? If you changed it, what direction would you take? As soon as you start talking direction and self-image, you're beginning to talk *vision*. A vision is the big picture about you. Your vision is your dream, your map of the future. It provides you direction. It is how you want to share yourself with the world. It's who you want to become, how you see yourself in totality. Your "big picture" vision can include other smaller pictures. Each picture is a vision of yourself, and collectively, they form a larger vision. Visions are different from goals. A goal is a destination that has very little emotion attached. A vision has passion and commitment; it's a heartfelt dream that stirs up your emotions. A vision encompasses many goals and transcends goals. A vision will not be denied; it has a life of its own. You pursue a vision with vigor to the point at which it is questionable whether you hold the vision, or the vision holds you. Straying from the path leading to your vision leaves you frustrated and empty. When you're heading towards your vision, you feel fulfilled because you are a visionary, transcending previous limits that restricted you from a full expression of yourself. In pursuing your vision, you will experience a lot of satisfaction; you'll experience emotional highs and a sense of well-being that comes from recognized achievement. This is particularly true if you recognize the achievement yourself.

A vision prompted me to write this book. Not only did it get me started, but it carried me to completion. My vision kept me on my path. One day while writing, I felt inspired and I intended to write several pages. I got an early start, only to find computer problem after computer problem. My frustration kept building and building until I started to doubt my competencies in many areas, including writing this book. By mid-afternoon, after six hours, I knew the book and I were both hopeless. It was evident that self-indulgent, negative self-talk had triumphed.

The next morning, my vision transported me back to my task, inspired once more. Magically, messages appeared on my monitor telling me how to solve my computer glitches. Visions are wonderful things; they have been described as radiating from the stirrings of our souls.

Remember, your vision is for you: be cautious in sharing it. Others may not consider your vision very lofty or inspiring, and their comments may detract from your enthusiasm. What is important is what the vision does for you, and how it provides meaning to your life. It is your perception of how you want to fit in the world, how you want to express your talents. It is a concept that involves you and fulfills you.

Visions work for a business as well as for an individual. To function effectively, a business needs a direction. Because a business can involve thousands of people, it is easy to see how a vision is essential to provide that direction. This became apparent to me when I was consulting for a venture capitalist firm. Every month I would review numerous proposals requesting an injection of capital. A proposal that was seriously considered always contained more than just a business plan and a profit goal. A venture with the potential to be accepted was always described in terms of a vision—a description of the big picture. The vision provided insight into the uniqueness of the business and detailed how it was going to serve its community. The vision also explained how growth for all concerned would be achieved. The whole proposal, besides being financially sound, was written in such an enthusiastic manner that I clearly wanted my firm to participate. Distilled from the vision was usually a mission statement describing concisely how the business would operate, or was currently operating, and how the business expressed its vision to all the people involved in its community.

Are you currently considering starting a business? If not, the following comments still have value for you as an individual. Whether you realize it or not, you are a business. Your business is how you live your life and make it satisfying and purposeful. Looking at how successful businesses operate provides insight for your own personal lives. The first step is to draft a vision for your business. From your vision, develop a statement about what the mission will be during the life of the business. You'll notice I said "life of the business." A mission statement describes more than just offering services or producing goods. Your individual mission statement will go beyond goals and contain your life's purpose. Individuals and companies must have a vision and a mission to be healthy, growing concerns.

Wanting to start and run a business was a vision that kept me working happily seventy hours a week. Those seventy hours were not all office hours, but I was *involved* in the business at least that many hours each week. Even when I was out skiing or hiking, I kept a notepad and pen handy to write down ideas. A good portion of my entertainment and recreation involved activities with compatible business clients. I was committed to doing whatever was necessary for the business to succeed. This included allowing time to fulfill my vision of family life, for if I faltered personally, the business would suffer, too. During those years my vision energized me so I could accomplish so much more and enjoy life fully.

Sometimes, being unable to achieve a goal will frustrate you. If you have a vision, your frustration will be short-lived. A vision carries you forward so you can establish new goals. Some people I know avoid setting goals, believing they then become too achievement oriented. Goals, they argue, prevent them from living in the present moment. This may be true, but I believe these people still have a vision. Their vision entails living in the now, with no thought for the future, and reacting to each situation as it arises. I believe that even a reclusive Buddhist monk, while perhaps living without a goal, still has a vision. His vision provides him direction, a way to live his life that is in accord with his values and beliefs.

"What do you want out of life?" I often asked this question of clients who appeared confused. It was a way to start building a vision, to start injecting renewed meaning and direction into their lives. Usually, they had many short-term goals that had not been met, and they felt lost. Without a vision—when goals are not fulfilled—you lack a sense of purpose and meaning. Goals give you the *how* of living, the means. Vision gives you the *why*, the purpose in living. When a goal isn't fulfilled, you just have to look for another how. You continue the pursuit of your vision. If your vision is to become a musician, one of your initial goals is to locate the proper teacher. If the first teacher does not meet your expectations, you don't give up your vision—you find another teacher and continue on. Later, perhaps you lack the money to hire the teacher, but this still doesn't stop you from becoming a musician. You look for another how in keeping with your vision and set another goal. Your vision remains intact, giving you direction so you can achieve what you want. In this fast world, a vision is essential to handling change effectively.

I've watched large corporations and governments lay off thousands of people. For many who were affected, the panic and fear was almost overwhelming, for they had no overall vision for their lives. Their goal was to work for the same employer until they retired. When they gave some thought to not working, common comments were, "I'm going to go fishing," "I'm going to travel," "I'm going to visit the grandchildren." You can imagine how devastated they were with the layoffs, because their future plans were activities, time fillers—not visions. Activities need to be interwoven with a bigger picture to form a vision, where they equip a person with meaning and purpose. The layoffs would not have been as bewildering if these people had been able to enlarge upon their activities and state them differently. Visiting the grandchildren could be revised to: "I want to become a significant adult in my grandchildren's lives. I want to watch them grow and share, so that my experiences in life become their legacy." The activity of visiting with grandchildren becomes part of how the larger vision can be fulfilled. Similarly, the fisherman could have said: "I want to communicate with nature and find out how I fit in the scheme of things while I meditate and fish." You may think I have raised fishing to a totally new esoteric status. Yet, every true fisherman I know practises living in the present, sensing the whole picture of life. It is just that most people who fish usually don't take the time to express what they're doing so descriptively. (I do enjoy fishing.)

You need more than just activities to feel satisfied about your life. Satisfaction does not lie in the activity, but in the purpose behind the activity. That is where you will find the vision. The vision provides the purpose; it's a description of how you want to grow and expand. It is how you will make more of yourself available to the world. For grandparents, there are many ways to share their legacy with their grandchildren, because their vision goes far beyond just visiting. People who fish—if they realize that the real purpose behind their fishing is to commune with nature—can do so without actually going fishing. That is the whole point: when you have a vision, you'll have many hows or activities to work with. If a life change denies your goal, you still have direction to get on with it. All it means is that you have to look around and find another how to move towards your vision.

The people who don't panic in the midst of layoffs have visions. The job they held with their previous employer is just *part* of their career vision. Their vision of work extends beyond their job, so they are not devastated when they are laid off. They may find it unsettling, but all it really represents to them is a relocation or redirection to where again they can share their skills and talents. After recovering from the initial shock, many of them see the event as an opportunity to more fully express their vision. The layoff is a chance for them to do something they have wanted to do for some time. They still have to make many adjustments, but they have a direction so they can continue to live meaningfully.

## Lay out your course

A vision is about you. To create a vision requires that you know yourself. When my marriage ended a few years ago, it was an enormous change for me. I had to ask myself, "How do I want to live my life and what is important to me? How do I envision spending the rest of my life?" I soon realized I did not want to spend my life alone. This then called for me to develop a vision for a new partner. I started the exercise by listing what I felt I deserved. All of a sudden it dawned on me—why not list what I wanted and desired in a partner? After all, it was a vision.

To accomplish this task, I had to examine myself deeply and decide on my values, interests, needs, and desires. It became a twofold adventure: one, to really get to know myself, and two, to draw up a vision. My vision needed to reflect who I truly was, without any facades, masks, or projections. This honesty was a liberating experience.

To be other than completely honest leads you down the wrong path. It serves no one, least of all you, to be modest or self-effacing. Go for it with enthusiasm and zeal. Remember, it is a vision and it's for you.

Lorraine, a nurse in her forties, delved into her inner feelings and desires when designing her life after her partner died. This is her vision.

*Whatever I do for the rest of my life, I do with love for myself, for humankind, and all other matter. I love passionately, without judgment and without investing in the return. I have integrity in all that I do. I know that I have wonderful things to do here on Earth, and I wait with patience and joy to learn what they are.*

*I am connected to every living thing with my Higher Self and with All That Is. I find information and mentors easily when I am learning and reaching for new tools and ideas. Ideas flow easily; they are wonderful demonstrations of love* and caring. I use my gifts of intuition and awareness to connect deeply with those who come for direction, and I provide them with many loving, supportive, holistic, creative, and exciting ideas for growing.

I live in simple elegance, with light, color, and music in my environment. There is ample room for the activities of my life, with beautiful spacious areas for friends, for work, and for play. There are plants, textures, and natural fabrics and materials around me. There are gardens full of flowers and delicious vegetables, herbs, and fruit. My environment, which includes ponds, waterfall, walks, decks, and lights, harmonizes with its surroundings.

My relationships are loving and supportive and fun; they flow easily into and out of my life with goodwill and caring. I have a sexual relationship with a male that is intimate and deeply satisfying. This man loves me and lives easily and joyfully with me. He understands my need to be independent and knows how to be independent himself. He is beautiful in spirit, personality, and physical appearance. He loves to be around people and is a wonderful host. He accepts my family and friends joyfully. He is independently wealthy and thrives on work and fun. He has experienced many things. He has integrity and sees the world as a loving, joyful place.

I am slim, strong, shapely, and sexy. My body is vibrant and healthy. I have energy, stamina, and grace. I look young, sleep five hours at night, and work at a variety of projects, enjoying them all with gusto.

I am fearless, breathing and releasing those feelings that have kept me frightened in the past. Money flows freely as I complete projects, demonstrate my caring, and fulfill my needs.

The process of writing a vision flows when you take it lightly; have fun creating your vision, for that is when you are most creative. When you were a child, you were probably at the peak of your powers of imagination. It helps in writing a vision if you can become childlike again. Try the approach outlined in the exercise "Looking into your childhood" to become aware of your ideas at this time in your life.

～

The ideas that this exercise stirred up were enough for Debbie to start creating her vision. She was a recently separated, thirty-year-old woman who became frustrated in her work as a secretary. The only thing she was definite about was that she didn't want to continue what she currently was doing. We talked for quite a while, and I asked her many questions, none of which seemed to give her any insight. I finally asked her, "What did you want to become when you were five years old?" Without a moment's hesitation she replied, "A teacher, a school teacher." To give her reply credibility, I administered several psychological tests. They all indicated that Debbie had the necessary abilities and apti-

---

**Exercise:** *Looking into your childhood*

1. On your notepad list all the things you wanted to be and do between the ages of four and twelve. Give yourself some time to do this, at least the greater part of an hour.

2. If nothing comes to mind immediately, put down the pen and paper, and while keeping the task in your mind, do something else. It may have been a while since you were in contact with your childhood dreams, so give them time to percolate to the surface. You may find that the ideas from this exercise are sufficient to start on a vision.

tudes to be a teacher. Acting on this information, she returned to university. When I saw her again, after seven years, she enthusiastically thanked me for my help. She went on to describe teaching as the most rewarding profession she could ever have envisioned for herself.

To develop a helpful, guiding vision, you need to reawaken your childhood imagination; wonderful things happen when you do. You may be a person who has disregarded a large part of your childhood. Allowing yourself periods of childlike behavior brings insight to many forgotten desires and dreams. Knowing these desires is essential to creating a meaningful vision.

Of course, you know yourself—but do you? How often do you allow yourself full expression during a favorite activity? How often do you take the risk of appearing foolish, by doing just what you feel like? When was the last time you allowed yourself the solitude to sit and daydream for an hour in a beautiful setting? When was the last time you felt such a need to release energy that you found a place where you wouldn't disturb anyone and shouted, actually bellowed to your heart's content?

Doing such things may seem totally impractical and unrealistic. Yet, they are simple things that allow you to express who you are and how you feel. It is so easy to lose touch with yourself in today's world by placing limits on your behavior. Sometimes you just need to let the little child out to reawaken and restore your creativity. Someday you—and all of us—will have to ask, "Was it worth it?" Let's make sure it was.

A meaningful vision requires you to be aware of the values, interests, and personality traits that are unique to you.

### Exercise: *Exploring your uniqueness*

Write down twenty things you enjoy doing. To help you start, here's a list of some activities, examples of lifestyle and interests.

Urban living

Rural living

Marriage and family

Travel

Leadership roles

Spending a lot of time alone

Socializing and entertaining

Meeting new people and hearing their stories

Telling others of your life story

Closeness with others, intimacy

Hiking and skiing

Water sports and sailing

Organized sports, either as a spectator or player

Running and jogging

Walking and ambling through nature

Sun tanning and lying on a beach

Gardening

Camping in a tent or recreational vehicle

Staying in a luxurious hotel

Attending live theater

Attending the symphony and ballet

Attending popular artists' performances

Attending art shows and exhibits

Attending church and religious functions

Attending or participating in horse shows or equestrian events

Pets and animals

Crowds and social gatherings

Teaching and showing others how to do things

Researching the Web for topical information

Creating your own web site

Building things; e.g., woodworking, stained-glass

Intricate work

Restoration and maintenance

Retiring from work as soon as financially possible

Working as long as possible

Reading fiction

Reading autobiographies

Reading and practising self-help concepts

Watching sitcoms on TV

Meditating and seeking spiritual growth

Discussing and listening to opinions of others

Debating and convincing others

Organizing and directing

Making and closing a business deal

Initiating new possibilities

Learning new skills

Being on the leading edge

The exercise on page 60 lists topics to help you explore and value your uniqueness and interests you often ignore.

This is only a partial listing of interests and activities but, hopefully, it gets you thinking. If you're still having trouble uncovering some of your desires, "expand your awareness" using the exercise on this page.

You may find that two items on your list are in conflict, or are mutually exclusive, but both interest you. That is quite normal and acceptable. Many people enjoy contrasts, which can be stimulating and energizing. Some people enjoy solitude, but they also thrive on being with people and attending social events.

My wife Joanne and I have a residence on a lake eighty miles long in the mountains of southeast British Columbia. Living there in the winter, the closest we come to another person is a fishing boat within half a mile of shore. The location is surely one of the most beautiful spots in the world. We find the quiet and the closeness of nature inspiring. Yet,

**Exercise:** *Expanding your awareness*

Answer these questions:

- What would you like to do if you had only six months to live?
- What did you want to do before you (got married, had children, bought a house, etc.)?
- What would you do if you had six months of paid vacation?
- What job can you do more effectively than most people?
- What accomplishment would you like to be best known for?
- What wish would you like "a fairy godmother" to grant you?
- What are the first three things you would do after winning a lottery?
- What activities would a company pursue, if you owned the company?
- What would you do if you were ten, fifteen, or twenty years younger?

we both enjoy being with other people, listening and sharing our energies with them. The two lifestyles are almost complete opposites, yet we find them complementary. We use the time by the lake for creating and recharging—it's a gestation period. Then we go to the cities to get "citified." It is a different learning experience, and we find it equally creative and satisfying. Most of us need contrasts to fully appreciate and benefit from life's adventures. So don't hesitate to acknowledge, enjoy, and fully exploit your opposite interests. That way there is more of you to share with the world.

**Exercise:** *Writing your vision*

1. Choose a time when you are at your creative best—when "I can't" has not become prevalent in your mind. If your circumstances prevent you from doing it right now, then do it in the next twenty-four hours, either just before you go to sleep, or on waking up first thing in the morning.

2. Write sentences that describe your vision. Write in the present tense. The vision needs to comprise all the important aspects of your life. The following is a suggested topic outline:
   - Describe how you express your creativity and share your talents with the world.
   - Describe your possessions and how you enjoy them.
   - Describe your physical health and activities that maintain a healthy body.
   - Describe your relationships, including family friends and business associates.
   - Describe how you experience and live each day.

To be complete, the vision needs to cover the physical, emotional, mental, and spiritual aspects of your life. As an author, I could state my vision briefly as:
   - I am enjoying my creativity by writing a book that encourages people to embrace life and all its experiences.
   - My life is abundant in all areas. I am provided with the opportunities I desire.
   - I am in excellent health, enjoying my current age. I am physically active, appreciating my remarkable body.

## The fun part: write your vision

With the information you gathered from the previous exercises, let's write out a vision. It doesn't have to be complete at this time, and you can add to it anytime you desire. Remember, though, for the vision to be valid, it must serve you, for when it serves you, it will serve others. Too often, visions are written on the basis of what would please other people. This vision is going to allow you to expand so, yes, it will please others, but it will also provide you with a deep sense of fulfillment.

- My friends and associates are very supportive of me, and my personal relationships inspire me to transcend boundaries I have imposed on myself.
- My life is exciting. I greet each morning enthusiastically, knowing that the day's experiences will further my growth.

Starting a business might be part of your vision; if so, use concrete terms and measurable outcomes whenever possible. Cover these areas in your vision:
- An outline of the service you provide to your community.
- How your service benefits your community and you.
- How you perceive your community and how your community perceives you.
- The size of the business and its growth rate in percentage terms by year for the first five years.
- Outside expertise required and the type and number of employees for each of the five years.
- The relationship you have with your employees and contractors.
- How you handle the transition of delegating the day-to-day welfare and maintenance of your business to others.
- Describe the first five steps you take in the next month to grow your vision.
- Continue with other characteristics of your business that you want to describe, although these will get you started.

Remember, your vision is not written in stone. You can change it or add to it whenever you desire. The key is to make a start and to get your mind focused on creative possibilities. Good luck and enjoy the process. You will probably find things you didn't know about yourself.

## Express yourself through images

The next step is to express your vision using pictures. The "Dream board" exercise will inspire you and help fix your vision in your mind. You will be creating a dream board or treasure map. You can collect the necessary images from magazines and other sources over a period of time, or you can draw them. Many people find it is best to set aside two hours when you can be alone and undisturbed to do the exercise. Don't in any way shortchange yourself by being inhibited, or feeling you are too adult for this sort of thing.

---

**Exercise:** *Dream board*

1. Take a sheet of posterboard (a fairly stiff sheet of heavy paper, approximately two by three feet) in a color you like.
2. Cut out images and pictures from magazines that represent the desires and activities you've used to describe yourself.
3. Paste these ideas of yourself on the large sheet.
4. Describe the images you have on your board with statements that affirm the activity/accomplishment and you. The statements can begin with:
   - I see myself...
   - I hear myself or others saying...
   - I feel and want to...

Choose any or all three of these types of statements—whatever suits you best. The idea is to make the statements positive with as much enthusiasm as you can muster. The number of statements is not nearly as important as the energy you feel when you express the ideas.

---

Have fun with the exercise and remember it is for you; you need not show it to anyone else. This is time for you to explore and play with your imagination.

## Allow your dream to unfold

Once you have completed these five exercises, you will have a new sense of accomplishment and certainly a new sense of direction. Likely, you'll feel some of the limits and restrictions that used to nag at you have moved further away. You will have much more room to express yourself and the energy to do it with because you are experiencing a sense of having made several decisions; the energy-robbing state of indecision is gone.

If starting a business is part of your vision, now is the time to develop the business plan and write a mission statement. A mission statement based on your vision is as important as your market research and the financial data in your plan. The business plan will define capital needs, timing, and other material requirements—for these requirements, it is quite appropriate to get professional assistance. The mission statement, though, is slightly different; it is your responsibility, because only you can state with the necessary accuracy what the true purpose of the venture is. As your business grows, naturally you'll want your employees and associates to join you in preparing a common vision and mission statement. But in the initial stages, you need to take the major initiative so that you're guided in putting together the most effective team.

Having a vision is like flying an airplane: you follow a course or flight plan. You stay on that course, unless something happens, until you reach your destination. When an intervening event occurs, you adjust for it. Sometimes the adjustment is slight and can be handled by an automatic pilot; other times you may have to land. Once you've dealt with the problem or challenge, you resume your trip to your destination.

Your vision is similar. In the event you lose your job, separate from a partner, experience bankruptcy, or any of countless other situations that can occur, you still have meaning and direction in your life. You now have a vehicle to create or handle change. At times you may get diverted, but you have a purpose and the means to resume flying. How high you fly depends on your vision and you. I wish you excellent visibility and unlimited ceiling.

Exercises in this chapter have given you insight into who you are and where you want to go. Recognizing your true value allows you to fulfill your vision. It's very difficult to receive a marvelous present when you deny that you deserve it. You deserve your vision. It came from within you; it is your unique creation. It belongs to you—now is the time to take possession of it.

Believing you deserve your vision paves the way for you to express it fully. The beliefs you hold generate the attitudes and perception you have about the world around you. In the next chapter you will understand the impact beliefs have on your life and uncover beliefs you didn't even know you held. You will find it exciting to discover how to change your beliefs and thereby change your world.

# Chapter 4

# Developing Supportive Beliefs
# to Empower Your Vision (*Step Two*)

Beliefs are habits of thought. You hold beliefs about every aspect of life: love, money, relationships, health, and work. Your beliefs determine your world. They define who you are, who you are becoming, and what you perceive your purpose is in life.

Your beliefs determine your actions. This became obvious to me one day when I spent a fascinating hour sitting in my car at a large shopping center in Phoenix. I watched people come into the lot, park their cars, and then leave them. I noticed that the drivers secured their vehicles in a variety of ways. Some would leave the car unlocked, some would lock the doors, while others attached a steering wheel lock before also locking the doors. After a while, I also noticed that the degree of security did not seem to be based on the model of the car or the length of time the driver was gone. It occurred to me it was a function of how the driver perceived the world.

Your perception of the world is based on your beliefs, and your beliefs are based on life experiences. For some of the shoppers I observed in the parking lot, the world was quite safe, and they didn't feel threatened. For others the danger was real; they felt vulnerable. It seemed as if those people were looking over their shoulders expecting someone to pounce on their car and steal it. Their beliefs—how they perceived the world—determined how they left their car.

Beliefs determine how much money you have and how you manage it. There are two common conflicting beliefs about money:

- Money is abundant and easily available to you; and
- Money is scarce and difficult to obtain; you must be extremely cautious with it.

As money represents or *is* really energy, your beliefs regarding this energy impact immensely on your life. When people live abundantly, it is because they believe money is available whenever they need it. They may have few physical assets and little money in a bank account, but they still feel money is readily available to them. You can easily spot their belief system by the way they use their money—they enjoy spending it without worrying how they will replenish it. They *believe* life is abundant, and they live it abundantly.

For others who believe money and the so-called good things of life are hard to come by, their belief is supported. It seems they never have enough. Scarcity is the byline of their life.

As a child, I worried about our family having enough money. Would we have enough food to eat? Would we freeze to death? The belief that I gleaned from my family was that having enough money was difficult to achieve. I also believed that those who had abundance were exploitive and took advantage of others.

I was in my late teens when I first met Al. Despite being raised in a family with very little income, Al had established a belief that financial success was easy to obtain. Due to various circumstances, he received a grade-three education and started work in his early teens. Apparently, at that age, he had not established any restrictive beliefs about abundance, or if he had, he was capable of adopting new ones.

Al's beliefs and behaviors were a shock to me. Why, here he was a millionaire with a grade-three education, who was well-liked and respected by his employees and associates. Contrary to my belief that if he had money he must be stingy and exploitive, Al was very generous, providing free rent for my young family when I returned to college. Al's belief that the more you spent the more you earned served him well, and he died a dearly loved, wealthy man.

Today I still feel indebted to Al. He provided such strong support that it was possible for me to hold beliefs that were different from the ones I had learned as a child. Without knowing it, he had challenged my childhood beliefs about scarcity. I saw that I could develop a new belief without feeling guilty of betraying my family.

## Transcend limitations

At the center of your personality are core beliefs. Many of these beliefs come from your parents and grandparents and many generations before them. The experiences that generated these beliefs happened so long ago they are now forgotten. Only the belief is remembered and passed on to you, the child. When you receive a belief without knowing its source, that belief is granted much more credibility. It takes on the aura of a *truth*. The type of truth that "just is" cannot be challenged. This is how beliefs reach the status of truths and the perception that they cannot be changed. You may have given many of your beliefs this written-in-stone status and taken them into the core of your being, without being aware of it.

Your core beliefs often pertain to moral issues or safety concerns. Parents repeat them many times, trying to impress their importance on their children. You may even have been expected to follow these beliefs without questioning them. Despite your parents' good intentions, sometimes your well-being and happiness requires adopting new core beliefs. Failure to do so leaves you unable to deal with the world effectively. It helps to realize that many of your beliefs are only appropriate for a given time, and that time has passed. Similarly, the beliefs may be based on a given set of experiences, and now they're being inappropriately applied to a different set of conditions. Society and the world change, and it's necessary for you to challenge existing core beliefs.

During the course of my life, I've changed many of my core beliefs—those relating to forgiveness, mistakes and failure, good and evil, and other basic morality issues. I used to believe that punishing myself was an effective way to alter my behavior. Life experiences and my counseling practice have shown me forgiveness and positive rewards are much more effective. I used to think helping others was a "good thing to do," that being "good" and "doing good things" was my purpose in life. Now I believe that what is good is a matter of opinion. What one group defines as good behavior, another group of people label as bad. I now see things as neutral—neither good nor bad. I approach situations with love and avoid judging. Significant shifts in my beliefs have had a profound effect on how I've handled my life. I doubt that I would have survived emotionally if I hadn't adopted these new core beliefs. I am very grateful for the help I received in making these changes.

Fearful experiences can also lead to core beliefs. The emotion connected to these traumatic events causes the resulting habit of thought to be firmly planted in your personality. Your phobias and irrational fears usually stem from these perceptions, making it extremely difficult to adopt a more functional belief. I know this from personal experience.

I almost drowned as a teenager, trying to swim in water that was over my head. Out of this experience grew my belief that I was in danger of drowning anytime I was in deep water. Now years later, after learning to be a more competent swimmer, I still have this fear. Slowly, I'm beginning to set that belief aside and experiment by swimming briefly in deeper water. I have taken up scuba diving to experience breathing underwater. By acquiring a broader range of exposure, I hope to establish a different belief about deep water. I'm getting there, but I still feel challenged.

## Uncover your beliefs

Often people ask, "How do I know what my beliefs are?" Frequently, you live life with little regard for your beliefs. They are such an intrinsic part of you that you just continue on your day-to-day routine. You do not doubt they are there; you are simply not conscious of them.

A good way to uncover your beliefs is to ask questions of yourself. The questions may pertain to a current situation or to a core issue or belief. For instance, if you are feeling and expressing anger after being cut off in traffic, the questions might be:

- Do people usually take advantage of me?
- Am I frequently a victim?
- Are other people self-centered bullies?
- Are people really aware of the impact they have on others?
- Is it a big deal or is this just a passing experience with no real significance unless I make it so?

The questions, you can appreciate, are endless, but they do uncover your beliefs. Some questions, though, probe to the core of your being. For instance:

- Do I really believe I'm a good person (or bad person)?
- Do I deserve to be loved?
- What is my attitude towards sex and marriage?

With this last question, do you hear your parents' voices providing you with a set of rules? Ask yourself, "Are these my beliefs or theirs?" I do not suggest you should reject your parents' values. But now may be the time to make sure the beliefs you hold are truly yours, and that you want to continue to hold them.

When you are taking charge of your life, good questions to ask are:

- Am I responsible for my life?
- Are my parents and how they raised me the source of who I am right now?

You may also consider a topic—for instance, money—and write down the thoughts you have about it. Usually those thoughts are aphorisms that were repeated to you. They could sound like this:

- Money doesn't grow on trees.
- Money is the root of all evil.

- Money makes the world go round.

Have fun with this. Treat it as a game of self-discovery. You may even find that many of your beliefs conflict with each other. This conflict leads to further discovery.

## Is it this or that?

Being human, you are often irrational. In fact, sometimes you even have conflicting beliefs. Whenever your behavior causes you to feel stressed or confused, that is the time to ask yourself what's happening. You will probably find that you have one belief that tells you to go ahead and another that drags you back when you start to move forward. No wonder you feel agitated; you're literally being pulled in opposite directions! If you continue long enough in this situation, you become stressed out and fall prey to many dis-eases— appropriately named, because when you're stressed, you have no ease. Stopping the stress-producing behavior only gives you temporary relief.

So when you're in a situation where you're experiencing a great deal of stress, ask yourself, "What beliefs do I have concerning the situation?" It is easy to discover the first belief. Then ask yourself, "What other belief do I have that opposes the first one?" You can also look closely at your actions to find the conflicting belief that is causing your stress. When you find it, you can adopt a new belief that grants you the necessary freedom. You will experience a tremendous feeling of oneness or wholeness that results when you own beliefs that support your actions.

Some female/male relationships provide wonderfully clear examples of conflicting beliefs. People claim to want harmonious relationships, yet describe their partner's failings and shortcomings at length to friends and associates. "She is impossible" or "He is so stupid." The "battle of the sexes" may be better stated as a "battle of the self." Conflicting desires introduce tremendous stress in our lives. Regardless of the opinions of others, it is time to step out on our own with beliefs that support our desires.

In life you are surrounded with beliefs. Eventually you need to take charge and select beliefs appropriate for you. If you don't, you will soon have many beliefs in conflict as your life experiences increase. You are not a mechanical robot, and soon your demands for growth will cause you to act in conflict with a belief. This conflict cannot be resolved effectively by simply changing your behavior. The only action that satisfies conflicting beliefs is no action at all. Some people try this approach and live in a depressed, limited state. This is not the route I suggest for you.

Sarah, a retired teacher, lived most of her adult life depressed. She lived with a married man who separated but never divorced. They had children and maintained a stable relationship for many years. All this time, though, she was depressed because of her two beliefs. She believed it was wrong for her and her partner to live together unmarried. Yet, because she loved this man and they had children together, she believed they should be together. Eventually he died. Her relief finally came when she met with a minister of her church, who helped her adopt a new belief—that it was okay for her to have lived with this man although they were not married.

It does not work to ignore your conflicting beliefs. To have peace, you need to address the conflict. The easiest way out is to adopt a new belief that reflects the action you desire to take, or the action you've taken.

Take a look at the "belief" prisons you create for yourself. You add a torture chamber to the prison when your desires and beliefs are in conflict. You get a sense that your desires are wrong, so there must be something wrong with you. You assume self-judgment and guilt. In many cases, the offending belief is one that attached to you in early childhood. The belief was appropriate for a child but not for an adult who needs to live responsibly in an adult world. Fortunately, your desires change as you mature, but often your beliefs stay trapped in childhood. After all, your parents gave the beliefs to you, and they didn't give permission to change the beliefs. You are unaware that it is you who must grant the permission. So you generate a lot of guilt when adult desires are unsupported by childhood beliefs. Often this is the source of guilt feelings in areas of sex and creative play.

Have you ever wanted to do something but felt it was wrong? Don't just ignore those feelings and brush them off—try to determine their source. Often the source comes from a belief that was appropriate when you were a child. As the belief surfaces in your mind, look at it and ask yourself this question: "Does this belief fit me as an adult, and does it express who I am today?" If the belief is no longer appropriate, give yourself permission to adopt a new belief. I suggest you have a little fun with this idea of inappropriate childhood beliefs. The next time you're feeling guilty, visualize one of your parents talking to you. Can you hear what they're saying? Are they telling you what you should do, what you should want? If you get that childhood feeling of powerlessness, it's time for you to assume your true adult role. Take responsibility for yourself and make your own decisions. You will feel empowered and your stress will vanish. Realizing that no one can impose beliefs on you without your permission gives a whole new view of the world. Suddenly, it becomes *your* world.

You can now be in command of your beliefs and fulfillment of your desires. You now have a way of reducing conflicting beliefs. You feel like a new person taking hold of your life; it does wonders for your stress level, confidence, and self-esteem. You start moving ahead guided by your desires, instead of being pushed by the shoulds of your old beliefs and without being dragged back by conflicting beliefs.

I remember working with John, president of an oilfield service company, who practised the following exercise very effectively. Whenever he experienced conflict of this type, he would have what he called "a team meeting with myself." When I asked him what this meant, he said that during the meeting he would take the role of a coach; the conflicting beliefs were the team players. As a coach he could decide which team member to put into the play and which play to execute. In his college days he had been a successful hockey player and transferred his sports experience to business. John was an effective manager and a good model for me to follow on changing my beliefs.

What a dilemma I had with my beliefs! I had been a supervisor for an oil company for several years when I decided to return to university and complete a degree. My employer was very supportive, offering financial support with no strings attached. Somewhere in my childhood I picked up the belief that companies abused their employees. In particular, I saw oil companies as exploitive, always taking advantage of their staff. Imagine the stress I was experiencing—I needed the financial help, but I knew there must be a catch. I really believed my employer had an ulterior motive. Somewhere, somehow, I felt I would have to pay dearly if I accepted their assistance.

After experiencing considerable stress, I realized I needed a new belief, one that stated my company believed in treating its employees fairly. The company really did want to create a win-win situation; that is, my working for them was because of desire and not because of a contract. I gained the insight that if I were to grow I would need to change some of my beliefs. It also helped me understand the "beliefs and desire conflict" and the accompanying stress. The stress was coming from inside of me and it really had nothing to do with anything external. The stress was my responsibility, and I had the means to deal with it.

Realizing that you have control over much of your stress is surprising. Whenever you feel blocked, depressed, and confused, check for a belief conflict. The same goes when you're feeling guilty or unworthy; it is a strong sign you have a "desire/belief" conflict. Knowing that this conflict is occurring within gives you all the authority you need to resolve it. Doesn't that make you want to shout "Freedom at last!"

You can experience that freedom if you're having problems with money. If you desire more abundance than what is present in your life, you can bet that a desire/belief conflict exists. You may want abundance and wealth, but your belief system says affluence is wrong. You are not alone; others hold this belief. "Money is the source of all evil" still rings true for many people. As a child, I frequently heard the saying, and often it still echoes in my memory. This is particularly true whenever I'm trying to fulfill material desires. A desire is something to be heeded; when it is causing stress, examine it. In the area of abundance, usually the desire is appropriate but the conflicting beliefs are inappropriate. Try adopting a new belief and you will be surprised what happens.

Nature will help you with new beliefs. Nature provides magnificent proof of abundance and yet still maintains a balance. Look at the beauty and the varieties of flowers and vegetation; they all exist in great profusion. The vast oceans, the billions of stars in the night sky give more than ample proof of nature's abundance. It follows then, if this bounty exists throughout nature, it must exist for you. You are a part of nature as much as any tree, plant, or star. So if you're lacking anything, it is time for you to adopt a new belief for yourself. Here are some suggestions you can use to build your own belief:

- I am connected to the source that creates all things.
- Having abundance is an expression of energy, and I am energetic.
- One of my purposes in life is to model abundance for others.
- The only lack that exists is in my thoughts.
- I accept abundance as a natural state of being.
- My desires are fulfilled by an abundant universe.
- I am part of an infinite universe that is always expanding.

You are at your creative best when you're having fun. So the idea here is to have fun creating a new belief and a new life. Enjoy—it's your life!

## Get into the driver's seat

Want to change your world? Here's how. You adopt a belief that supports the new world you desire. Usually, you don't adopt that new belief with a snap of the fingers. While it is as simple as that, old habits and fear get in your way. The first step is to suspend any old beliefs that prevent you from making the change you want. You then look to see what new beliefs would support the change. Next, experiment behaving as if the new beliefs already exist. It helps if you can take on a playful mood, engaging your imagination and sense of humor. Assume the role of an actor and see yourself acting in a play. This is what Mark and Ellen did when they came to see me with marriage difficulties.

Mark and Ellen had both outgrown their old beliefs. Mark was an engineer who had his own successful consulting firm. He had been raised in a family with a nurturing, yet controlling mother. In his early forties, he had matured in many ways but still held onto his childhood belief that men were dependent on women—hence, his dependence on Ellen, his wife. Mark was no different from many other people who tend to fear and want to control the person they depend on. Outwardly, he had the appearance of the stereotypical dominating male.

Ellen, also in her early forties, had recently returned to work as a pharmacist. In Ellen's family, the father was dominating and at times physically abusive. Ellen's mother survived the relationship by appearing to be submissive, but controlling through subtle manipulation. Ellen believed that men were to be feared and could not be approached directly. She believed that she had to make her wants and desires known subtly and trick men to do her bidding.

Mark and Ellen had been married for fifteen years and away from their original families for more than twenty years. As they had both matured, family influence was waning. Mark now wanted a partner who was more an equal and a peer. His belief about being dependent on Ellen made it truly difficult for him to stop trying to control her. He was stuck. He didn't realize that to fulfill his desire he needed a new belief. Ellen had desires similar to Mark's. She had grown to the point of not wanting to "sneak around." She also wanted a partner and an equal for a husband. However, her childhood belief about men blocked her from fulfilling this desire. So there they were, both blocked and frustrated with each other.

They each believed the solution lay in the other person's making major changes. Ellen stated unequivocally that she could no longer tolerate Mark's controlling behavior. Similarly, Mark said he could no longer live with Ellen's manipulation. He was tired of guessing her needs and wanted her to "stand on her own two feet and be straight" with him. They each knew the other partner had to change and had lots of evidence to prove it.

Initially, the idea that childhood beliefs were the source of their problems sounded ridiculous to both of them. They were sure their problems had nothing to do with their own individual beliefs. The cause of their grief lay in the behavior of the other partner.

I started with asking them individually to imagine how they would behave if the problem was solved, then to decide what belief each would have to adopt to support that behavior. All through the process, Mark and Ellen were encouraged to focus on themselves, not on the other person—because you can only change yourself.

The second step was for each of them to recognize they did not have to fear the other. Naturally, neither was willing to admit to this fear. So all they were asked to do was to describe how they would behave if they were to be vulnerable to each other. Could they be more responsive to one another if they believed they were capable of handling each other's behavior?

For Mark, it meant believing that he wanted Ellen as his wife because he loved her, not because he depended on her. Similarly, he needed to believe Ellen was his wife because she loved him, not because he controlled her. This meant Mark had to recognize that he was strong and capable enough to deal with Ellen on an equal-partner basis. He no longer required "the upper hand" to be Ellen's husband. Ellen also needed new beliefs that recognized her strength—that she could deal directly with Mark and no longer feel it necessary to "come in through the back door." This meant acknowledging her value as a partner and not just as a subservient "yes-dear" wife. She needed to adopt a belief that her value derived from who she was rather than what she did for Mark.

Experimenting is necessary to adopt new beliefs. Fortunately, both Ellen and Mark had the courage. They were willing to bring some humor into their situation and try some role-playing. They each practised "If I believed such and such, this is how I would act."

The role Mark invented for himself was one of an independent male capable of caring for his domestic needs. His first experiment involved washing his dirty clothes. Both of them found it amusing, particularly Ellen, as she explained to Mark how to operate the washing machine.

Ellen also had her work cut out for her. She chose the role of a woman who expressed her desires so others would have an opportunity to give. With good humor, she used the idea "it's better for them to give than to receive." She saw herself sufficiently capable of giving without diminishing herself or her resources. Ellen loved back rubs, so her first risk-taking request was that Mark give her a massage.

In our conversations, we did not dwell on their fear, but instead looked to their strengths. By becoming aware of their strengths, they both realized they were more capable than they thought. Both of them discovered they had sufficient resources to deal with any challenge that came up in their relationship. They could actually test their new beliefs—it was okay to be vulnerable with the other partner.

Each of them designed an experimenting schedule for themselves. In Ellen's case, once a week she would express one of her desires directly and openly to Mark. Once a week, Mark would focus on one area in which he felt he was totally dependent on Ellen. He would develop a strategy and then use it to handle the need independently of Ellen.

They both continued their conscious role-playing and testing for a couple of months. Initially, they checked with me weekly, and later, every two weeks. Then we waited for three months before the next session. At that time, they were elated at the progress they had made. No longer did they have to role-play; they had both adopted new beliefs and, as a result, enjoyed a new relationship. Their revised beliefs about each other had also started to generalize, so they could deal differently and more positively with all members of the opposite sex. It was a rewarding demonstration of how to change beliefs.

Many snarled family relationships come from outdated beliefs. Often you will hear family members telling each other: "Well, you always..." Such statements suggest the speakers have not updated their beliefs to recognize change in themselves and others in the family.

Two sisters, Mary and Doris, demonstrated this clearly. They were having a lot of trouble with each other. Their present relationship was based on old childhood experiences and beliefs that would not allow them to accept each other as they really were. They both desired a closer relationship but did not know how to achieve it.

To solve their dilemma, they needed to suspend their old habits of thought. When they worked on the problem, they found "new eyes" to see the woman that each of them had become. Their story goes like this.

Mary, being older, had often corrected and advised Doris when they were children. Now they were both mature, competent women, and Mary no longer felt responsible for Doris. Mary desired a relationship based on equality rather than "Mary-knows-best." Often she complimented Doris on her accomplishments, but Doris took these remarks as sarcasm and ridicule. She was grounded in the old childhood belief that she couldn't do anything right in Mary's eyes. Doris would not allow the new data to be interpreted to form a new belief. She responded by commenting nastily on Mary's accomplishments.

Rather than moving closer together as they matured, the two sisters were growing apart. To change the situation, each sister would have to adopt different beliefs. When Doris suspended her old belief about Mary's comments, she was able to respond in new ways. Mary then responded differently to Doris and reinforced Doris's changing beliefs. Rather than enduring a relationship of put-downs, they became very supportive of one another.

~

Often people don't have the open support of others in altering their beliefs. Jennifer, a former client, had this difficulty. As a baby, she had been abandoned. The family who adopted her perceived her as a burden. Jennifer interpreted their actions to mean she was unworthy of their love. If you define love as a connection between people, you will understand why Jennifer felt so alone. Because she felt unloved, she also believed she didn't have the capacity to give love. She felt inadequate. If she had something to offer to others, wouldn't she be receiving love already? Despite the desire to connect with others, people usually avoid admitting it. They feel this protects them from any further hurt.

Jennifer was an excellent example of this behavior. In her job she provided care to physically handicapped people, whom she believed would not have the emotional strength to reject her. The care she gave was extremely proficient and appropriate, but mechanical, offering little warmth. Thus, Jennifer minimized her emotional risk. It also meant she lessened the chance of receiving positive feedback from her wards. They responded to her in a similar cold manner, reflecting her fear.

Despite her reluctance to admit it, her strong desire to give love and connect with others saved the day. In our sessions we focused on this fact, and Jennifer began to realize she really had something to offer others. Furthermore, she recognized her need to receive love. She was then able to take more risks. She developed a warmer manner towards her clients, they responded favorably, and Jennifer began to feel appreciated.

She became happier and her joy spread to the relationship with her partner. Previously, Jennifer had been frustrated in the relationship, threatened by her partner's acts of love and desire for intimacy. She lashed out, at times being physically abusive. Jennifer found her own behavior bewildering. Here was a man she loved, but when he demonstrated his love, she became so fearful that she abused him.

Jennifer's life started to change when she examined her belief that she was unlovable and had no love to give. Acting on my suggestion, she was able to suspend her old belief and do some experimenting. We felt it was best for her to experiment at work where the relationships were less intimate and less threatening than at home. I first asked Jennifer to imagine she was a very loving person and had a lot to offer the people in her care. I did not ask her to reject the old belief but simply to suspend it temporarily. During this period of suspension, she would act in this new caring way. As a result of the experiment, the clients reflected love and appreciation. Jennifer now had the necessary information to build a new belief—that she was a lovable person who knew and could express love.

Despite falling back for short periods on the old belief, Jennifer persisted with the experiment. Soon she no longer needed to suspend the old belief; she had a new one. Naturally, this created for her a new world that carried over to her personal relationship with her partner. She had established a basis on which to accept his love and interpret his behavior positively. She no longer felt a need to react from fear when he offered her intimacy and love.

⌒

This beautiful healing story showed me the step-by-step process for adopting new beliefs and revealed the extent to which beliefs have power over actions and perceptions. When we know how to adopt new beliefs, we choose our own dance in life and transcend boundaries that have restricted our growth.

You can appreciate from Jennifer's example that adopting new beliefs is not a mechanical one-, two-, three-step process. It is the process of moving forward, falling back,

---

### Exercise: *Adopting new beliefs*

1. Using simple words, outline to yourself a new belief you'd like to adopt; for example:
   - I am able to give and receive love.
   - I am financially secure.

2. Think of how you will behave according to the new belief. Write this new action in simple, brief statements; for example:
   - I do loving things for others.
   - I accept compliments easily.
   - I tithe ten percent to charity.
   - I pay my bills on time.

3. Start acting out these new behaviors by role-playing, if necessary. Every time the old belief surfaces in your mind, say to yourself, "I suspend this belief temporarily." You can tell an old belief has surfaced when you hear your inner voice warning that your new action is wrong or that you cannot do it.

4. Continue experimenting and checking how you feel about this new behavior. Is it giving you the results you desire? Remember that you can always change your actions to achieve more fulfilling results. Similarly, you can modify your new belief so it is more fitting for you.

This is an experiment; you have only temporarily suspended your old belief, which you can fall back on anytime you desire. During this process, it is extremely important you realize you are in control. You set the speed at which you change. The new beliefs are your own creation and completely under your direction.

and progressing again. For the sake of explanation, though, I describe the process as a step-by-step forward procedure in the exercise "Adopting new beliefs."

Be aware there are triggers that cause a retreat into the past. They pop up when we behave as if we are operating under the old beliefs. I often found myself regressing when I visited my mother. She would ask me to do an errand for her, and I would feel resentment building up in me. I felt under her domination, and I needed to struggle for my independence. Today, I realize what was going on and wish I could explain to my deceased mother that my behavior had nothing to do with her. She was witnessing a forty-year-old man behaving like a teenager, acting out beliefs he held in his early teens. When I moved my focus back to the present, I behaved like the adult rather than the teenager. Oh, what a relief!

## Ready, set, go!

Imagine yourself being very fluid and responsive to events in your life. Your stress level is low, and you feel totally free. This happens when you know how to change your beliefs. You can act as the situation demands, and that can change your total perspective on the world. You can change who you are, who you believe you are, and what you perceive to be true. Initially, you may react to this suggestion with fear. You may feel that if your beliefs are not fixed, you will not have a stable base to make decisions. When an event occurs, you won't know what action to take. You are afraid you will have an identity crisis; you won't know who you are. Actually, you will be able to respond much more effectively and be more constructive. However, your identity *will* change; you *will* become a happier, more successful person. Sounds like a good deal to me.

Going one step further, imagine what would happen if you had a belief that was appropriate for every situation. You would be creating a belief to fit the situation, rather than forcing a certain situation to conform to your existing belief.

Often we try to get situations to conform to our beliefs by denying reality or blocking our awareness. I see this happening frequently in what I call "tests of love." Children of separated parents, partners in a relationship, and older parents with mature children commonly use these tests. They say, "If you loved me, you would..." They believe love can be expressed in only one way, and if not expressed that way, it isn't love. Similarly, people will tolerate enormous abuse because of inappropriate beliefs. In both situations, the "victims" have beliefs that are fixed and absolute. Their world would change if they could generate beliefs to fit the situation; there would be no need to deny events, and they could become more fully aware and alive. They provide good examples of how a change in beliefs comes first—before the change in reality occurs. When we change our belief, we are free to see a new reality.

Personal growth requires that you *believe* you can change your beliefs. Unless you have this basic belief you are stuck, and change is very difficult—in some cases impossible. As stated earlier, beliefs define your world. If you cannot change your beliefs, your world is static. You become rigid and you cling tenaciously to old beliefs, despite demonstrations from the world around you that you need to change.

I often hear clients say, "This is how I was raised" as an explanation for their behavior. To me this means that they are failing to regard themselves as adults and to take responsibility for who they are right now. Granted, how you were raised is certainly an important contributing factor; childhood experiences do impact on who you are right now. But, that does not have to be the final and complete answer. If you do not take responsibility for the current situation yourself, it means you have no control in your life. If you want freedom, you have to take responsibility for who you are.

You create your world and are responsible for it. When I first heard this statement, I was angry. How could I be responsible for my parents' separation and for being raised in a financially limited situation? After I spent a week examining this idea, my anger faded. I realized that if I wanted to direct the events in my life, I needed to take responsibility for it. That was a tremendously freeing idea. What it said to me was that I could determine what direction I wanted my life to take. What liberation from my old thinking! Previously, my beliefs had confined me and restricted me to continue a lifestyle similar to the one I was raised in. I am truly indebted to the statement that got me thinking that day.

It takes courage to be willing to change beliefs. Usually, you'll find you are going against popular opinion. You may feel as if you're trying to swim upstream against the current. You may be accused of being foolish. To be a willing change-master doesn't mean you are spineless or lack values. It means that you are willing to adopt new beliefs that work for you as new situations develop in your life, and this places you in control. You are deciding who you are and how you will act. This doesn't mean you have to reject all the values and beliefs your family bestowed on you in childhood.

Instead, you are free now to select which of those beliefs fit you. You are also free to change them in the future if you feel it is appropriate. Beliefs need to be fluid and dynamic, for then your energy soars. You become the director of your life.

⁓

Let's review the process of changing beliefs:

1. You change beliefs by creating new ones that are more appropriate.
2. You avoid a frontal assault to your personality by requesting a temporary suspension of the belief you want to examine.
3. You bring in new data to see if the old belief is still valid.
4. If a new belief is appropriate, you can adopt it.

The key to this process is to avoid judging yourself wrong. You simply develop a new belief by leaving the old one sitting there, no longer being energized by your thoughts. During the initial period of suspension, you test the waters by moving away from the old belief in stages. You seek experiences that gently challenge the old belief. You gather new data as you gain more confidence and progress to greater challenges, modifying the belief to what fits for you. In time, if you don't put the suspended belief into play, it simply fades away. Like a plant that has been starved of water and nutrients, the old belief dies.

When I swam in deep water, I didn't start trying to change my beliefs by swimming laps in a pool that was over twelve feet deep. Initially, I swam only a short distance where the water was over my head. Gradually, I increased this distance, building my confidence while I developed my new belief. This is the easiest and least stressful way to accomplish the change process.

Occasionally, life demands that you demonstrate new beliefs in what feels like an instant. Perhaps you have said to yourself, "I would never live with a woman/man who..." But then you find out that the person you are attracted to does that very thing! You are caught. Perhaps your children confront you with behavior you have declared unacceptable. What do you do? The necessary switch can be completed easily if you have already given yourself the freedom to change beliefs to fit your needs. You are free to make the appropriate decisions and take action spontaneously. There's none of the agonizing, critical debate with yourself. You just do what's necessary without further thought. It's wonderful, isn't it?

During the period of changing your beliefs, it is very important to monitor your self-talk. Observing what you tell yourself is important; otherwise, you may sabotage establishing new beliefs. To observe yourself and be aware of your self-talk usually requires considerable focus.

Often, with clients, I would use a visualization exercise to help them hear their self-talk. I would ask them to visualize being in a theater listening to themselves on stage. What script were the actors—the clients—using for the drama they were playing? This was a wonderful opportunity for them to realize that they were writing the script; so they were free to change it.

The same holds true for you and me. We write the script and we are free to change it. No more negative self-talk!

## The power of positive talk

To counteract your negative self-talk, those undermining statements you repeat to yourself, you need a positive statement—an *affirmation*. Use the affirmation that strengthens the new belief, yet does not reject the old belief or imply that it's wrong. It simply states the new belief.

An affirmation moves your attention from what you don't want to what you desire. It gives you a positive focus because it is impossible for negative self-talk to continue when your mind is occupied with stating an affirmation.

Singles who lose a partner through separation or death often need to change their belief if they want to start a new relationship. Affirmations are very helpful in this case. Often there is a lot of fear in seeking a new partner because beliefs have been established based on previous relationships. If a past partnership was satisfying, people often believe they will never find another as gratifying. I have often heard the comment "What's the point in trying?" Yet, people desire and crave the companionship to be found in a new relationship. A helpful affirmation is "I am a good partner and I know how to select a good mate." Keep in mind that the prospective partner will be different from the previous partner. To have a meaningful relationship, an acceptance of difference is necessary. Remember, to find the same relationship is impossible and denies the prospect of achieving an even better relationship.

There are also affirmations for those who previously had an unfulfilling relationship. Many of these people feel they are incapable of selecting appropriate partners; they keep recalling the pain of the past. So for them, an appropriate affirmation would be "I now know what I want in a partner, and I now can choose a marvelous mate."

Finding myself single after a growing and satisfying relationship, I used the following affirmation: "I've had a good relationship, and I will now find an even better one." Initially, some people felt that I was denying my grieving process. I wasn't. I was simply confirming my desire to have an even more fulfilling relationship in the future. The affirmation was to support the necessary belief.

Share your new beliefs and affirmations with caution. This is particularly true when people don't share your values and perception of life. When you tell others, you will sometimes receive expressions of dismay and criticism. Oddly enough, this is especially true of your friends and family. They all love you dearly and want the best for you. They want to keep you "safe." This usually means they want you to avoid any changes. They are afraid that using these positive affirmations is an invitation for you to get hurt. What they do not realize is that languishing in an unhappy situation results in even greater emotional pain. Don't let others—or your fear—control you. Affirm what you desire and allow life to let it happen.

## Live a full life

If growth is important to you, start choosing beliefs that allow you new experiences. You are a practitioner of life and life is a learning experience. A great affirmation to start the change process is "I now choose beliefs that serve me well." I developed this affirmation with assistance from a personal coach when I was working on a marketing project. I was being blocked by old beliefs from my teen years, beliefs that reflected my inexperience. Yet, I had become a different person; I was more knowledgeable and better informed. I had something worthwhile to offer the world. My affirmation of flexibility helped me market myself. The new beliefs allowed me to contribute my talents more effectively to society.

So whenever you want to embark on a new adventure, you must look at your beliefs. Are they congruent with the purpose of the adventure? Do they fit? Will your beliefs allow the adventure to be a constructive endeavor for you? If not, why not change those beliefs? Why not adopt beliefs that will support you in the adventure?

The need to develop new beliefs was very apparent to me when I worked with groups in therapy, helping people design changes in their lives. It was necessary for them to examine their existing beliefs and how the beliefs contributed to the life they were leading. Next, they would look to see if they could adopt a belief that was more useful.

Many of the people came to the groups feeling "I'm a victim." We would look at how that belief resulted in their actually being victimized. Often, they found they were creating situations in which people took advantage of them. They wore the body posture of a victim—collapsed shoulders and an aura of lethargy—indicating to more aggressive individuals that these people felt defeated and vulnerable. Before long they would be victimized again.

Some people in the groups would seek revenge and victimize others, then experience the consequence of being "victimized" again when called before the courts. In their opinion, the court was the aggressor and they were the victims. The belief that they were victims sometimes won them sympathy, but never freedom. Freedom came when they changed their beliefs. They first needed to believe that they had something to do with their situation. Recognizing they had a responsibility, a choice in creating their condition, they then had the power to create a different situation. The essential ingredient for making a shift in their life was changing their beliefs.

When you are looking seriously at redirecting your life, it helps to grant yourself some latitude in changing the beliefs you hold. For instance, if you are dismissed or laid off from a job, you might believe you have been dealt with unfairly. Your mindset becomes one of victim. Until you adopt a new belief, your "victim" thinking restricts you in seeking another job. First, you feel powerless. Hence, you lack the energy to begin a new career search. Second, feeling victimized because of a past event means you are living in the past. You cannot find a new job in the past; you must do that in the present. Optimizing your chances of getting new work means developing a belief regarding your victim state.

I was once laid off during a corporate cutback and felt disempowered and victimized. It wasn't until I changed the belief that I was a victim that I became mobilized to start a career search. I would sit out on a viewpoint of the city and say, "In all of those buildings, somewhere there is a place for me." This belief, used as an affirmation, brought me many successful career adventures. I gained knowledge and experience accompanied by financial rewards that previously I would have thought impossible.

Whenever you feel blocked, examine your beliefs and find out what they are. See how they affect your life. Ask yourself, "What beliefs do I have?" Then see how they are creating your world and impacting on your life. This is an amazing way to get to know yourself. Once you have these insights, you can take control of your beliefs and your life. Remember, you have chosen your beliefs, and now you can choose again.

Choosing beliefs that serve you well is an effective way to live. It puts you in the driver's seat. This means steering your own course and becoming empowered to live a full life. You can live a life in which your energy is directed towards fulfillment of desires and expansion of self. In turn, you contribute in harmony to an ever-expanding universe.

Once your beliefs harmonize and support your dream, you are ready to move to the third step of change. How you view yourself will determine if you manifest the energy for completing the transition successfully. When your self-concept is strong and energized, you can effect change that is appropriate for you. The next chapter provides exercises that make you aware of the capabilities and strengths you possess.

# Chapter 5

# Discovering the Treasure Within
## (*Step Three*)

Closely connected to your vision is your self-concept. While your vision gives you direction, your self-concept decides whether or not you will fulfill your vision. Your self-concept is the foundation on which you build your life. It's critical then that your self-concept is strong enough to allow your vision to be realized. In this chapter, you will explore your self-worth, the roles you play, your skills, your uniqueness. You will learn the art of self-praise. The discussion and exercises in this chapter provide a way of leading you to restoring your natural self-confidence and developing your self-concept.

Consider your self-concept as a diamond with many facets or sides. Each facet represents how you see yourself in relation to somebody or something else. You see yourself differently in relation to your partner, your children, your parents. You have a concept about yourself regarding each of those relationships. You also have a self-concept when it comes to a myriad of activities, whether it is speaking in public, going to college, practising your profession, or running your own business. Collectively, all these views of yourself contribute to your self-concept.

Your sense of self-worth is an integral part of your self-concept. If your self-concept is a many-faceted diamond, your self-worth is the value you place on the diamond. It is the value you place on yourself, whether you consider yourself worthy of changes, whether you respect yourself and believe you deserve the outcomes that you desire. Your self-concept creates your internal world and determines how you react to your external world.

Knowing this, the next step is to develop a self-concept that is appropriate to fulfill your desires. When changes are occurring, you will make decisions based on your self-concept. Starting with your sense of self-worth, let's probe deeper into seeing who you truly are.

## Realize your value

Looking at how you came into existence is one way of gaining an appreciation of you as a person. You have your own beliefs in this regard, but I do know that there was something outside you that led to your existence on this planet. That something—whether you call it God, Life Force, or Universal Energy—valued you enough to cause your existence. The very fact that you exist says you have value. This idea was brought home to me one day when I was cross-country skiing in a beautiful mountain valley. I was awed by my surroundings, struck by the thought that the same process that created this beauty had created me. It made sense to me that I, too, must have beauty and worth. My value stems from my very being; this realization is the basis of my self-worth. Naturally, what applies to me applies to you.

What a waste it is to disregard our value. It means we deny the world our talents; we deny the full offering of our being to society. When we don't fully appreciate ourselves, we shy away from giving what we have, what we do, and what we are. We're afraid of criticism, afraid that other people assign a lesser value to our being than we do. As a result, we undervalue who we are and deprive the world of our true nature. Even more important, we deprive ourselves of the joy of full expression.

If we look at ourselves as part of the universe, an integral part of all there is, we recognize we have a worthy part to play. Otherwise, why would we be here? There must be a reason. We know the universe does not tolerate waste, does not allow chaos—nothing is random. Time and time again, our scientific community has demonstrated that there is order in the universe. Our life, this existence that we call ours, has worth and purpose. There is something we need to do, and we need to value ourselves in order to deliver the goods. If we don't value ourselves, we are "under-living."

Suppose you were at a banquet and a starving child approached you for some food. You would not hesitate to feed the child. Yet, if you don't value yourself sufficiently, you are denying those in need. You live in a world that is starving for what you have to offer. And if you evaluate yourself honestly, you will realize that you can offer a banquet.

You may not be a grand pianist or a world-class tennis player; you may not be a well-known politician or the owner of a fleet of trucks, but that's not what you're called on to offer the world. You're called on to deliver what you have—but first of all, you must appreciate what you have. You must recognize your value, realize that what you're worth is immeasurable. You are all-right!

What worth do you place on yourself? One way to find out is to ask the following questions:

- Do I value myself enough to change my behavior?
- What about worry? Do I value myself sufficiently to stop that behavior?
- What about guilt? Do I value myself enough to release any guilt I may harbor?

It's fine to acknowledge that your past behavior is not what you want to repeat today. But you need to value yourself sufficiently to forgive yourself and release all guilt. Otherwise, those guilt feelings will restrict you and block you from behaving constructively today. You need to affirm: "I value myself sufficiently that I let go of any guilt I have about my past."

The next step is to start giving thanks for the incidents that triggered the guilt. Your experiences have enriched you as a person and given you insight into how you want to change your behavior. You now have more to offer the world.

Without life experiences, both positive and negative, you have only potential value. Your experiences realize that potential; they give you value, not only for the world but for yourself as well. Experiences are assets, and as you appreciate your assets, you start appreciating who you are and further develop your sense of worth. To derive the greatest value from your experiences, you need to give thanks for all of them.

## Love your uniqueness

Often we try to realize our uniqueness by comparing our-selves to others, which is dysfunctional and meaningless. It undermines both parties. We may be comparing one of our weaker traits to one of the stronger traits of the other person. Yet the balance could be completely reversed if we were to compare a different character trait. The truth is all of us have individual character traits that humanity values and needs. Comparisons—accurate comparisons—are impossible because of our uniqueness.

In our society, where everyone is equal, we get confused. We tend to view "equal" as "same," yet sameness and equali-ty are two different measures. In North America we all have a vote, which is the equality part. The fact that no one can vote in our place and that each vote is counted demonstrates our uniqueness. If we were all the same, one person could vote for all. We forget that we count as individuals. It's sort of a paradox: we are all different, yet in many ways we all have a similar value. For instance, if you were lost in North America and your location was known, you would be res-cued within twenty-four hours, weather permitting. This is regardless if you were a millionaire or on welfare, if you were known to millions or only to your family, if you were an infant or a mature adult. Every possible attempt would be made to rescue you. You have value, just because you are; you have value because of your uniqueness.

What is so important or significant about this unique-ness? The answer is that no one can take your place in the world. You can search all over, but no one can fully replace you. In business we often hear the phrase "You can be replaced." It is false. Someone *can* do your job but never exactly in the way you do it. What you bring to the world no one can offer or duplicate.

Recent attempts at cloning animals support this fact. After a few years of "successful" cloning, scientists are finding the clone is not a true clone. They are discovering unique traits that are present in the gene donor but absent in the clone. Even if science becomes totally proficient at cloning, the donor and the clone will still be different by virtue of the dissimilar environments they have been exposed to. Environments affect all living organisms; to a degree we are products of our environment.

Identical twins are an excellent example of this difference. The twin born first, even just moments before the other, is always perceived to be the older one. In many families this minute difference is treated as if it were months. This isn't the only factor that creates difference. Being held in opposite arms of the same parent gives each child a different exposure. Frequently, the babies are cuddled by different parents or people outside the family. They will never be exposed to identical environments. Regardless of their similarity, the twins are unique and different. What you do with your life, the people you influence, the things you create or modify are unique.

The footprints and fingerprints you leave on the world can never be exactly duplicated. Every time you explore a new spot or have a new experience, it is virgin territory relative to you and the territory. You have never been there before. What is equally important is that the place or situation will never be the same again after you have been there. You will leave your mark, your energy, your essence. This thought is awesome. Each day you are going to change and have impact on an environment that has never been impacted by you before. What a wonderful challenge. What a glorious opportunity.

The value we place on something is based on its availability and how plentiful it is. Seeing that you are one of a kind means you are priceless. You have a once-in-a-lifetime opportunity, a unique job to do. You cannot avoid impacting on the world, so why not impact in a way you desire. Your input will be lost unless you express your desire, your individual motivation. You may ask, "Is my desire appropriate for expression?" The answer is that you will never know unless you express it. It will only be inappropriate if it results in a consequence you do not want. If that happens, you can always adjust your action and experience a different consequence. But consider the possibility that the resulting consequence is exactly what the situation needs. When I supported clients in expressing their desires, they would say, "What if people laugh at me?" My answer: perhaps humor is what is needed at that moment.

## Restore your natural self-confidence

Yes, you need restoration. It's not your body or your hair— it's your self-esteem. When you were born, you had no doubts about your capability or your worth. You were a "natural." You expressed yourself spontaneously and had an abundance of self-confidence. Somewhere along the way, most of us learned to fear many things and question our worthiness. Some of us even heard that we were "bad," or at the very heart, base and sinful. It's no wonder that many of us became boastful, aggressive, and abusive—that was often the only way to gain a sense of personal power and a feeling of worth. We all know there are better ways, and for some the process means a lot of pain and suffering before this is realized. So let's take the easier and more joyful route. Let's look at restoring the belief that we are worthy and capable of fulfilling our desires. Let's replace "I can't" with "I can" and take our natural place in the world.

Recently, I witnessed a beautiful example of this sense of self-worth. I was watching a demonstration of Highland dancing when a little girl, two or three years of age, left the audience and spontaneously joined the dancers. She went out and danced as if it was the natural thing to do. The audience was delighted. We could all appreciate the importance of believing in ourselves and having the self-confidence necessary to express that belief, just as she did. It was a joy to watch and learn from this little girl.

So, maybe it's time to expose the little girl or boy in you. It's that part of you that is enthused about life and wakes up every morning excited about what the day might bring. You don't question whether you can handle the changes that might come; you just welcome them as opportunities to learn about life. How old were you when you felt that way? I was four years old, and I can still recall my excitement about life and my belief that anything was possible. I didn't see anyone as having super powers; I just saw them without limitations. I believed also that when I reached adulthood, I would be free of restrictions and limitations. That sense of power is still available to both you and me today.

Take a moment to reflect right now. Go back in your memory to a day when everything went just right, whatever you needed appeared, and everything, including you, seemed to fit in the world. Now renew a sense of how you felt on that day. You will find you have the same feeling as when you were the child. Enjoy the feeling and let it pass when it's natural to do so; avoid trying to hang on to it as if it were a scarce commodity and not readily available to you. In reality, it has never left you from the time you were born. It is normal for you to be self-confident; it is just that fear, shoulds, and false morality restrict and deny your natural self.

Nurture this feeling of confidence when you're experiencing change. Know that one way or another, you can handle whatever life grants you. Remember when you were a child and you didn't know how it *should* work out, so you went ahead and did your part. You followed your script in life's play without worrying or telling yourself "I can't do this." Remembering the childhood joy of unabashed self-expression is one way of restoring your natural sense of self-worth.

Once you have recalled that good feeling about yourself, it is time to build on it. Gather information about your current capabilities, strengths, skills, and traits. Doing this helps you realistically appreciate who you are.

Lori, a thirty-year-old retail chain store manager, based her assessment on the twelve years since she had graduated from high school. Before she completed the exercise, she felt she was woefully lacking in skills. She had focused so intently on improvement that she didn't realize she had already grown significantly. Lori said that while some of her skills were completely new, many were old skills that she had developed to a much higher degree over the twelve-year span. Completing the exercise increased her confidence for further growth. This is her list:

1. Learned how to present myself more positively with

personal grooming, body posture, facial expressions, and dress.

2. Learned how to listen to people and hear their needs.
3. Learned how to be persuasive and present my opinions assertively.
4. Have higher-than-average math skills.
5. Acquired up-to-date marketing strategies from recent business courses.
6. Learned how to reduce conflict and introduce calm into a situation.
7. Learned how to cooperate with others and develop common goals and game plans on how to achieve them.
8. Learned how to bring together my personal and work life more effectively.
9. Developed a sense of humor and the ability to laugh at myself.
10. Learned how to accept compliments and be more open with others.
11. Learned how to lead and help others organize themselves.
12. Learned to accept that I'm not perfect, but that it's okay, and I'm becoming someone different.

When Lori finished her list she reflected on how she and others had benefited from the skills she acquired. She knew her customers trusted her and saw her as a reliable resource in meeting their needs. Her staff viewed her as an effective mediator who was interested in their welfare. Management believed she was deserving of her bonuses and store awards. Lori also realized how her increased skill levels had benefited her and her family. She was now comfortable in expressing love and being vulnerable in ways that she couldn't have imagined twelve years earlier. She knew she had matured into a successful person, one that was still becoming. This prospect excited her.

Now it is your turn to appreciate yourself. Use the exercise below.

Another way of determining a more accurate perception of yourself is to review what you call your failures in life. Once when my self-esteem was at a low ebb, I made a list of "failures" that turned out to be successes. (See exercise "Listing sucesses.") I remember feeling like a complete failure when, part way through the term, I dropped a math class at university. Looking back, I realized it was a great success, because it was one of the few times I had had enough self-confidence to say no to something that was inappropriate. I recalled another instance when I got a mediocre raise in pay, yet my co-worker (who I thought did not perform as well as I did) received a much larger raise. Later reflection helped me understand that this "failure"—not getting a bigger raise—was what led me to a much more rewarding job elsewhere. Each of these so-called failures turned out to be the launching pads for great learning experiences. In writing my

**Exercise:** *Assessing skills and abilities*
1. List the skills, traits, and strengths you have acquired from these various areas:
   - Education
   - Work life
   - Friends and associates
   - Other skills that I possess
2. Now list how you have put those skills to work for you, and how you and those around you have benefited from your actions.

list, I realized I often overlooked the strengths I possessed, the skills that could turn these failures into successes. The exercise also helped me see that by making changes, I had created opportunities for myself. This realization boosted my self-esteem.

When we get trapped in negative self-talk it's helpful to go outside of ourselves. This allows us to get information on how others perceive us and appreciate us. The exercise "Gaining another perspective" on the next page helps you gather information outside yourself. Try it.

There are other exercises you can do to increase your self-esteem. However, all the exercises will fail unless you value yourself enough to accept positive input. Sometimes to allow this to happen, you must understand that accepting positive input is the opposite of being on an ego trip. What you are doing is equipping yourself to be of greater service to the world. The more you can do to enhance the creation you call "you," the more you can offer. Accepting valid praise and positive input is a win-win situation; everyone including you benefits more from your life.

**Exercise:** *Listing successes*

1. Make a list of your successes, or what you originally thought were failures but later became successes. Start with the first time you heard, or told yourself, you had failed. Remember the feeling, the emptiness in the pit of your stomach.

2. Now consider that event and the changes it created in your life. Invariably, you will find that eventually you used that "failure" as a springboard to greater success.

3. Continue to recall events and the subsequent successes until you have a minimum of three.

4. Appreciate how those failures were actually gifts, blessings that groomed and cultivated your beauty, producing the person you are now.

This approach often breaks through the barrier of self-doubt. There is a myth: "I am a better person if I deny self-praise and self-appreciation." By acting out the myth, I am indulging in a state of false humility or martyrdom. This is a misinterpretation of the concept: "The meek shall inherit the earth." I finally got this straightened out when I saw myself responsible to something outside myself. Then I was inspired to accept positive feedback and use my capabilities for greater accomplishments.

The key is to raise your self-esteem to a level where you can make the necessary changes in your life. Once you start making those changes, the process grows on itself. You make a change and that accomplishment feeds your self-esteem, which in turn prepares you for making further changes, which again nourish your self-esteem, and so the cycle continues. Your growth is perpetuated by further growth and there is literally no limit to your accomplishments except what you impose through your imagination and your vision.

---

**Exercise:** *Gaining another perspective*

1. Ask four people you know and respect—preferably not family members—to give you a list of skills they feel you possess.

2. Ask them to list the ways they have seen you use the skills in the past.

3. Ask them to list the ways they think you might be able to use these skills in a different way in the future.

4. Review the lists and appreciate how accurate they are and how they reflect who you are.

## Discover the Platinum Rule

Many of us have developed the belief that the way to improve, grow, and become more effective is to constantly point out to ourselves our "mistakes" and "faults." Nothing could be further from the truth. Most of us do not realize the extent to which we undermine ourselves through self-criticism. We have made a habit of self-talk, and the content is often critical. "Why didn't I...? I'm always...!" When we tackle a challenge—and life has many challenges—the last thing we need is to be undermined with negative self-talk.

An example I use in counseling to demonstrate the effect of self-criticism involves climbing a mountain with a pack on your back. Just before you start the ascent, you put a few rocks into the backpack. Then as you climb, every so often you stop and add more rocks. As you near the summit, it becomes debatable whether you can complete the climb because of the weight of your backpack. Indulging in self-criticism when you're adapting or making changes in your life is similar to adding rocks to your pack when you're

**Exercise:** *Monitoring self-talk*

1. Stop several times during the day to check your thoughts. Are you praising yourself or criticizing yourself?
2. If you are being critical, look for an area where you can truthfully praise and support yourself.
3. Compose a sentence that supports you. Examples are:
   - I accept and welcome my mistakes as a sign of my growth.
   - My imagination inspires me to accept new challenges, enabling me to offer new talents to the world.
4. Now repeat the sentence you have composed at least five times to yourself. If you are alone, it's even more beneficial if you can say the sentence out loud.

climbing the mountain. Each time you criticize yourself, you impede life's process and make it more difficult. How often have you questioned yourself with "Why was I so dumb?" or "How did I imagine I could do this?" These questions accomplish nothing except to decrease your energy and weaken your ability to make changes. Are you aware of your self-talk? Try the exercise "Monitoring self-talk."

It is miraculous how this exercise will increase your ability to accomplish change. I call this practising the Platinum Rule. The Platinum Rule is "Treat yourself as you would have others treat you." Another way of describing it is "Become your best friend." Practise this with a little humor; it can be an enjoyable process to enhance your effectiveness. We all become more effective with praise, and you're no exception to this rule. Please enjoy!

See yourself as a work in progress. Accept that you are continually evolving. The change you are experiencing has nothing to do with your being deficient or incapable. Instead, these changes or events all occur to offer you new experiences. They are opportunities for you to grow and to become a greater person, a person with extended boundaries and fewer restrictions. You can dance in tune with the universe, an ever-expanding entity.

When you allow yourself this perception, you see life and yourself through different eyes. You understand that how you complete a task or handle a situation is a learning event. If you had known how to do it perfectly, you would not have accepted the task, as there would have been no challenge for you. All these challenges move you along your path of growth. To criticize yourself for your "mistakes" is inappropriate and harmful to your self-concept. It is important to see mistakes as learning experiences. During an interview,

Edison, the inventor of the lightbulb, was asked about the hundred failures he had experienced before his invention was perfected. He responded that he now knew a hundred processes that would *not* produce a lightbulb. If we could all view experiences as providing that kind of vital information, we would not beat on ourselves when what we change does not give us the result we want. All of these experiences allow us to collect data that help refine our actions and choices.

The only error you can make in this regard is if you fail to see yourself as a dynamic being, always in a state of change. Remember, as long as you are breathing, you are in the process of developing and changing. Until there's no more life in your body, there's no stage at which you are a finished product. When you accept this fact, you will realize that there's no basis for self-criticism. When the criticism ceases, you will be surprised how easy it is to greet change with confidence. Your self-esteem soars, and you start learning from past experiences at an increased rate. They become a basis for your growth rather than a source of regret or a magnet tempting you to live in the past. You start applying the learning to the emerging experience. This process gives you a sense of competence that continues to lead to greater levels of self-confidence and a feeling of satisfaction from your accomplishments. Your life is like building a house. You start with the foundation and proceed with the next stages, the floor, the walls, the roof. The stages in your life are your experiences, on which you keep building. Each experience acts as a springboard to the next, until your life is completed.

I believe there are few universal rights or wrongs. History has shown us that what is appropriate at one time can be most inappropriate at another time. If you contemplate an act and it feels right for you, I encourage you to go ahead and risk. Perhaps you're the pioneer who will create a breakthrough for humanity. A pioneering act can be very simple. History has recorded that such things as a smile, a frown, a handshake, or a few words have started a chain of significant events. Look at the effect you can have by choosing to say "I love you" instead of "I hate you." Either phrase will have an impact on the recipient. You definitely can impact on those around you. You can affect the world in your unique way.

In relationships, our behavior has significant impact. It is a common source of how we undermine ourselves. When relationships are ending, clients often react by criticizing the departing partner, not realizing that in doing so they are being self-critical. They forget that they chose that "deplorable" person as a partner in the first place. The criticism is really directed at themselves for choosing to associate with such a person.

The next step in this dance of self-criticism is to decide what they personally did wrong in the relationship, which further decreases their effectiveness in finding a suitable new partner. When they focus on what they did wrong, they just increase the probability of repeating it. A more constructive reaction would be to look at what they learned in the past relationship and use this information in being a more effective partner in the next.

Georgia, a thirty-six-year-old teacher, came to see me when her second marriage was in difficulty. Georgia's mother had been very critical, believing one of the ways of showing love was to point out the faults of her children so the others could "improve." Georgia learned her lessons well and, in her first marriage, duplicated her mother's behavior. Eventually, her first husband left the marriage feeling he could do nothing right.

When Georgia came to see me, she had a full understanding of what had occurred. What she didn't realize was that in her second marriage, her "constructive" faultfinding was being directed to herself. Her self-talk became critical, resulting in her feeling disempowered and unworthy of her partner. She feared losing him and became very controlling. The resolution of the problem lay in Georgia's ceasing all criticism and studying the positive traits she possessed.

In our first session, Georgia and I discussed how her first marriage had prepared her for more fulfilling future relationships. She focused on how she now possessed more knowledge and skills in how to make a relationship work. She went on to further appreciate what her mother had taught her about the lack of praise. She was then prompted to make a list of traits she valued in herself and her new partner. Her next step was to use the list to praise both herself and her partner on a daily basis. After a few weeks of experimenting this way, she marveled at how it had changed her relationship. She had not thought it possible to feel so much more positive about herself and to have her partner respond so favorably. She had created a rewarding change for herself, all with honest praise.

I identify with Georgia because I've had similar experiences. One of the greatest difficulties in my second marriage was criticizing myself for "failing" in my first marriage. Today, it is a different story. My wife, Joanne, thanks the women in my past relationships. She firmly believes what makes me a "wonderful partner" is that I recognize and use what I learned from my past relationships. She also encourages me to thank my former partners for those learning experiences.

Many marriages, I believe, are meant to last a lifetime. Some of these are beautiful partnerships, in which there is love and respect and mutual support for growth. Other marriages, though, finish before either partner dies. When this occurs, it is healthy if the partners acknowledge the end and terminate the marriage. Then all parties concerned, children included, can make changes to build a more productive life. New relationships can be developed between the separated parties which foster greater growth for everyone. When those involved eventually become thankful for the past relationship, growth accelerates. The "failed" marriage takes on a whole new character; rather than being an encumbrance, it becomes a blessing. The previous partners can then be appreciated for the value they gave to the relationship. Everyone wins as they absorb enhanced feelings of worth. This is the self-image needed to effect change.

The material to build this positive self-image is immediately available. You find it in recognizing your uniqueness, the special print that you leave wherever you go that no one else can duplicate. You build this esteem when you recognize that your skills and traits are a unique blend that is you. You build with self-praise and self-respect so you are energized to handle the magnificent opportunities that change presents.

Another step in becoming masterful at handling change involves fully appreciating the process. Chapter 6 explores the transition so that you can engage change without feeling lost. Understanding what is going on gives you greater confidence in following the path that leads to desired solutions—the path that extends "onwards and upwards."

# Chapter 6

# Dancing Through Transition

Are you now convinced that you take an active part in the changes in your life? First, you choose your reaction to what happens. Second, when you are focused on fulfilling your desires, you play a conscious role in creating many of the shifts. Whether you have instigated the change or it is the result of another event, the actual process can be broken down into three steps:

1. You prepare for the event.
2. You allow the shift.
3. You embrace your accomplishment.

Compare the whole process to a trip. If you're prepared, you can sit back and enjoy it. Upon your arrival, you can take advantage of all the new opportunities. This being a human process, it doesn't fit precisely into compartments, and there is spillover from one aspect to another. Nonetheless, the actual change—the trip—is easy. Preparation requires that you accept the change so you are sufficiently motivated to get ready. Let's briefly review acceptance.

## Accept the events

You may find acceptance difficult when you've had little or no control over the change that has happened to you. Yet, as mentioned earlier, you still have choices. Your choice is deciding whether you will resist and fight change, or accept and work with it. For example, you will have difficulty finding fulfillment in a new relationship if you don't accept that the first one is over. If you have been laid off, you don't invest in job-hunting until you accept that your old job no longer exists. You accept the original change for two reasons:

- It exists in your reality; and
- You can learn about it and take whatever action you desire.

Resisting doesn't help the process; it moves your focus and energy away from working out a solution. The answer then is to accept change whether you like the change or not. Then you can get on with it and become involved in creating what you want. Be gentle and show compassion towards yourself when changes are not to your liking. Accepting what you don't like is initially scary. Does it mean that if you accept the change, you are stuck with it? Behind the fear lurks the thought that if you resist hard enough, the change will be reversed. But now you see that does not happen. During this time of acceptance you may have emotions that need to be expressed. Chapter 2 contains techniques for releasing your feelings.

We also resist because we feel it's an acknowledgment of a failure on our part if we accept something we don't like; e.g., marriage breakdown, loss of job, business collapse. We think if we block it out, it doesn't exist. We create a false reality. Yet, as soon as we accept the change, we can start creating a new life for ourselves and move on to more satisfying experiences. To make this adjustment takes time, and I believe it is part of our learning curve here on Earth.

Despite the myriad of changes I have experienced, I still get caught. Initially, I judge the change, and then I have to work at it awhile before I accept it. Finally, recognizing that each change is part of life's adventure reduces my stress and contributes to my happiness. Yet, mainly due to habit, I am not ready initially to just accept change without some protest or resistance. I still want to shout, "Wait, someone changed my program!" Then I ask myself, "Do I like it?" Along with everyone else, I need to remember that change is an indication that I am alive and, as long as I'm alive, I am being challenged. And life is a superb challenge in which growth always awaits you and me.

Okay—you have accepted the change. The next step in preparation is getting ready for the period of transition between the old and the new. This is where support comes in. We have already looked at building internal support through self-esteem and a sense of self-worth. Now it's time to look at a more visible means—support groups.

## Find your supports

Two criteria are most helpful in forming your own support group:
- Gather people who believe in you.
- Choose people who believe in the change you are undergoing.

If these are people who have successfully achieved the change themselves, so much the better. Their own experience will indicate when and how to support you. They also make effective models for you: the fact that these normal human beings have accomplished what you are attempting will strengthen your resolve. You will know it is possible. The most productive support group meets on a regular basis. Confidentiality is a necessity; the more trust that exists within the group, the more effective the group is. Naturally, the members focus on solutions and how to accomplish the changes, rather than problems and why the changes are necessary.

I have participated in several groups of this nature. In one instance, the only factor common to all the members was a belief in this process of change. The actual changes we were making and what we desired varied greatly. One member wanted to reconcile his feelings towards his alcoholic father and establish a new constructive relationship. Another member—as mundane as his desire might appear—wanted to learn how to operate a piece of heavy-duty machinery and use it freely over the summer months on his acreage. Both members accomplished their goals beyond their initial dreams. Usually, desired changes have much more in common than these two. I mention them to demonstrate how diverse and effective a support group can be.

I learned a tremendous amount as the facilitator of another group. These senior ladies were supporting each other in adjusting to major changes in their lives. Many had lost the companionship of a partner due to death or physical infirmity. What these women accomplished was nothing short of miraculous. Together they literally moved "emotional mountains." They demonstrated vividly how effective an external support group can be to someone who's experiencing tremendous change.

Another important element of support is your own personal reward system. Knowing what bolsters your spirits and turns you on is a great help during transition periods.

## What motivates you?

Your answer to this question is vital. It tells you how to construct internal support for any changes you are making. You need a payoff, a reward to keep you moving forward while you pass through that gap between the old and the new. Knowing what particular reward suits you helps construct a payoff system. It may surprise you to know that a payoff always existed in your old situation. You were rewarded for the past condition, or you wouldn't have tolerated it until now. So the new payoff you create must help you let go of the old and motivate you to carry on to the desired change. Let's take a look at some examples demonstrating payoffs.

**Situation 1**— You have difficulty accepting compliments and praise, and you want to change.
- Old situation payoffs: You projected inferiority, so others would try to rescue you. You denied your abilities, allowing yourself to perform at a less challenging level.
- New situation payoffs: A feeling of empowerment. A greater sense of freedom and independence.

**Situation 2**— You have been living alone, and now you want a partner, someone you can live with.
- Old payoffs: Greater personal freedom. Familiar, comfortable lifestyle.
- New payoffs: Joy of sharing. Possibility of greater support, new friends, and experiences.

**Situation 3**— You are an employee of a firm, but now you want to start a business of your own.

- Old payoffs: Predictable income. More shared career responsibilities. No capital risk. Less responsibility for other employees.
- New payoffs: Open-ended income based strictly on your success. Increased freedom in almost all areas and the potential for greater satisfaction.

**Situation 4**— You have been at your current position for ten years, and you'd like to branch out in a different career.

- Old payoffs: Current job is familiar. Socially, you know your work group and network. You have a proven work record.
- New payoffs: Exciting, fresh challenge. Chance to meet people. Opportunity to grow and learn.

When you're considering a change, make sure the reward for the new situation exceeds the old. Only you can decide the payoffs and their importance, because they are unique to you. A meaningful return is one that responds to your particular needs, values, and beliefs. Knowing these parameters about yourself, you can construct your own payoff matrix. If the reward for the new situation does not exceed the old, you need to closely examine if you want to make the change. If the answer is still yes, then you must re-evaluate the values you're placing on the individual payoffs. It may be that there's a part of yourself you failed to acknowledge before. Fear may have kept you from honoring values that are important to you—recognizing these values can increase your anticipated returns. This occurs as you allow yourself to be much more expressive.

It is extremely helpful, too, if during the transition, you

can plan on rewards at intermediate stages. Suppose you want to quit smoking. Plan on rewarding yourself after one day, three days, a week, and so on, until you're definitely a non-smoker. You then gain satisfaction from the money you saved and celebrate your healthier body.

Remember your vision—it is a great motivator and support. Whenever you're having doubts about the wisdom of the change you are making, reflect on your vision. It will give you direction and re-energize your waning enthusiasm. You can also experiment and have fun with your vision using imagination and role-play.

## Play your new role

Part of allowing your vision to happen is to imagine how you would feel and act if the vision was fulfilled. It is a tremendously constructive way to dance through the gap or transition zone. Imagine you are living a new reality, the reality of the vision you hold for yourself and your surroundings. If your vision includes greater wealth, an example of role-playing is to frequent places where people live luxuriously. You may want to visit the lobbies of expensive hotels, window shop at boutiques and other places that display items you desire. Abundance, though, is not restricted to wealth and spending money, so you can enlarge on this role-play to other areas you perceive as fulfilling.

Douglas, a man in middle age, was looking for new experiences. He'd always wanted to learn how to sail, so he began visiting marinas. In his mind he played the role of a sailor, seeing himself in a boat out on the water. On his third visit to a marina, he enjoyed a conversation with an elderly sailor.

The sailor asked Douglas to help him sail his boat; in turn, Douglas would learn how to sail. They spent many happy afternoons together on the sailboat. This partially fulfilled Douglas's vision. The following season the boat owner died, and his widow thought it only fitting that Douglas take the boat. He graciously accepted, appreciating how completely his vision had been fulfilled.

Giving thanks for your current situation and for your imagined reality is a great way to accelerate the arrival of your vision. Openly act with joy and enthusiasm, as if your vision is really your life. The one condition—if your vision is about having more money—is that you do not start spending money you do not possess. Going in debt or spending funds you don't have is not expressing abundance. I repeat this warning because I've witnessed many people encountering financial trouble this way. There are many aspects of a role-play you can assume, however, without causing difficulty for yourself. Use your imagination and treat the role-play as an actor would in a movie.

Some people I know role-play their vision on a continuous basis. One is an actor in amateur theater who loves to be on stage. He's a fantastic actor, but on the street he can barely say hello because he's so shy. When he adopts a character in a play, all the stops come out and he embraces the role. Another is an engaging minister in a metaphysical church who addresses over a thousand people on a Sunday morning. He states he is extremely shy, but he also says, "I tell myself that when I step into my role I'll function like an extrovert." And an extrovert is what you get; it's beautiful to watch. There he is, an agile seventy-year-old, hopping up and down from the stage. Role-playing allows him to live out his vision. If you are having difficulty going through this phase of change, or feeling your vision, pretend, "I'm a salesperson selling myself." Act the role out!

If you do adopt a role for a period of time, you will notice a gradual change in your reality—in your belief, your behavior, and your environment. Soon the once-dreaded change is a *fait accompli*—a wonderful accomplishment—and it's been achieved without pain, without all that self-criticism about your fear, and without that defeating phrase "I can't." People tell me they've accomplished many changes this way with ease and fun. When you enter into role-playing as if it were a game, it's enjoyable and constructive. Remember all the curiosity you had as a child. Become that child again, and let your life unfold.

Roles have other dimensions, too. Often when we get promoted in jobs, we feel we have to be someone else to fill the role. Nothing could be further from the truth. In fact, we've taken on the new position because of who we are, not because we will become someone else. We bring along the talent and energy of who we truly are, and people believe we are able to fulfill the demands of that role. We may have to learn additional skills and make some changes, but we need to maintain our essence when we assume a new role.

Becoming a parent for the first time is a major transition. Many couples I have counseled have had difficulty with this change because they think they must become totally different people. Suddenly, they feel they have to leave all their humanness out, their being, yet that is what the child needs so desperately. Fathers in particular believe they have to become disciplinarians, that they should behave a certain way because now they are parents—and they must "teach" that child. Children, though, learn best from modeling. So parents offer most to a child by allowing who they are to define themselves as parents.

Similar to role-playing is self-observation—it's like watching yourself on stage. As you observe, you can see if you like what's going on. Do you like your behavior? If not, change it. Remember you are writing this script; you retain complete control of how you react to the gap-transition period.

For many of us, it is a chore to wrap our minds around this idea. As children, we were dependent on our parents and had very little control in our life. We were not given the freedom to decide what we liked. In fact, many of us were told what was good, what was bad, and how to react to a situation. If we reacted in what was deemed an inappropriate way, we were corrected. Many of us hang on to this feeling that we are still not in control.

But stand back and look at who is responsible for your life. If you are accountable for your life—and you are—then control must be available to you. Otherwise, it's as if you are riding in a car, responsible for how the car is being driven, yet not allowed to touch the wheel. Life is never like that. If you are responsible, you are deciding on your life's direction. Often due to the stress of the change you are undergoing, you forget who is in charge. Your life is in a state of flux, and you may feel it's out of your control. Since you can't make wise decisions without information, observe yourself. This is the time to make adjustments; it is most critical that you take the wheel and steer where you want to go. It is your trip—literally.

## Wait in the void

Are you ready to let go of the old and allow the new in? Are you prepared to lift the anchor of your sailboat and drift for those moments of dead space before the wind catches the sails? You hold your breath and ask, "Is it going to happen?" It feels like an emptiness, a void. But it isn't really. Things are going on, action is occurring—it's a transition period. Now is the time to focus on making space for the new. The transition period allows you to release all attachments to the old situation and visualize how you want the "new" to look.

Remember Mark and Ellen, who needed to adapt to each other's growth. You can appreciate the feelings of uncertainty they had as they experimented with new behaviors. They asked themselves, "Can I afford to be this vulnerable? Can I really trust my partner will not take advantage of the situation?" Using humor and play in their experiments helped them cope with their transition period.

Dave, a client who had lost his leg in an accident, found that things around him started to have meaning when he focused on the present moment. Patience and curiosity were his allies in handling this period of strangeness. Patience allowed him time to heal, and curiosity renewed his interest in what might happen and how he might cope with his new body. I found both of Dave's strategies very effective for me in dealing with a terminated marriage. Patience helped me open my eyes and participate in what was happening around me on a day-to-day basis. My curiosity engaged me and had me wondering how and when a new relationship would unfold and how my vision would be expressed.

Starting a new business created a different emotional space for me. During the period when I was the only employee, it all seemed very strange. My comforting thought was that this "void" was a sign of growth. This encouraged me to be patient and view this time as the preliminary stage of the fulfillment of my vision. Telling myself that it was okay to be alone at this point and seeing I was capable of doing what needed to be done was very helpful.

Being comfortable with yourself is important at the transition stage because it's a new landscape without recognizable landmarks. It's what's called the "here and now"; the only thing that is known is what exists in the immediate moment, and it's always changing. The gap-transition can be a confusing time. On a rocky journey, the best way to avoid motion sickness is to relax and be patient. Patience is the keyword, patience with yourself and all those around you. Remember, you have prepared for this, you have all the support you need, and you've mastered change in the past. Now is the time to enjoy each moment and focus on the present. Many recovering alcoholics I have worked with have shown me the reward of being patient. It's gratifying to watch them negotiate this transitional stage successfully. Most of them have been active in the 12-Step Alcoholics Anonymous program. Their motto, A Day at a Time, can be reduced to a couple of hours or even a minute. Living in the present moment dissolves stress and encourages patience. Living moment to moment allows you to realize that's all you have, and most important, all you need. You can celebrate your aliveness and bask in a sense of wholeness while still in the process of becoming.

## Take it easy

During the process of change, slow and steady wins the race. You need to go slowly enough to be fully aware of what's going on around you, to maintain your support system, and correct your direction as you go. When you are stressed and anxious, there is a tendency to panic and move faster than your support systems can handle. You might also put your head down and lose your awareness, failing to see alternative paths to fulfill your dream. Take it easy and maintain a sense of confidence, knowing your vision will be fulfilled.

This is a realistic feeling of confidence. You have done the proper preparation by letting go of the old and being open to the new. You have a belief that facilitates change and you monitor your self-talk so it is positive and supportive. You have outside help, and you pace yourself to maintain that support. Now is the time to enjoy the gap, the transition from where you are to where you want to be.

Whether your change involves starting college or a new relationship, switching professions, or handling a $100-million deal, you'll benefit greatly by treating yourself to a healthy diet and exercise. The stress of change makes it easy to neglect this part of self-care. Ideally, perform your exercise outdoors—perhaps walk for half an hour a day, any time of day and in any locale, keeping in mind your own personal safety. Walking outdoors not only gives you exercise, but connects you with nature, something greater than yourself. You see change everywhere and realize that everything is evolving. This does wonders in placing the change you are experiencing in proper perspective. You can see that everything has direction and a purpose, similar to your vision. You can appreciate that nature goes through many transitions and successfully accomplishes change. It is easy to conclude that what you're doing is normal and, with persistence, your success is a given.

Now is not the time to procrastinate; a healthy self-care regime is as important as your vision to get you through the process of change. You deserve it! And you cannot have the best unless you're treating yourself well—enjoying life and knowing you have so much more to offer the world. If you follow these suggestions, the transition period becomes not just a time of waiting but an adventure. When you're in transition, remember the curiosity you had as a child. Awaken that curiosity to stand in awe on the threshold of unfolding. You can hardly wait to get out of bed to see what the day will bring. May you enjoy it, because you can never walk exactly this way again. Getting there may be so much fun that achieving your desired change will be anti-climactic. Nonetheless, take a moment and give your process of change some closure, so you can get the maximum benefit from your achievement.

## Celebrate the achievement

Achieving your desired change is like reaching the summit of a mountain. You're prompted to ask, "What's next?" But before you start the journey to see what's beyond the next hill, take in the scenery at this point. Catch your breath, check your equipment, and make the necessary repairs and alterations. You need to look at what you have accomplished in making your change. Allow this accomplishment to give you a sense of satisfaction and competence. Let your confidence build and relish the knowledge that you have the freedom of choice and the capability of change. You will understand that depending on situations outside of yourself for security doesn't work. Security is an internal thing; it's knowing that you can handle one way or another whatever occurs. With each change you experience, your sense of security will increase and you will master greater challenges.

As you realize you have more to offer the world, you will also notice that the world has more to offer you. Your horizons have expanded; you're no longer limited by old boundaries. You can now appreciate that life is a process and that being an unfinished product is exciting. Even when you experience moments of frustration and feelings of being blocked, you know there's a solution.

The next chapter examines some solutions to feeling blocked. You will discover how to redirect yourself to grow and extend beyond where you are today.

# Chapter 7

# Can't Dance? Feel Blocked?

You are poised for change, but nothing is happening. You feel you must be blocked because your vision is not unfolding as it should. Yet, your vision is clear and your desires are strong. How could you be blocked?

The answer to this perplexing question came to me in a dream I had several nights in a row. I was walking along when suddenly an immense brick wall blocked my path. I tried my best to climb the wall without success. I pulled the bricks out to dismantle the wall, but I was stymied again. Each night, my frustration and feeling of defeat woke me. Finally, one night, I faced the wall and stopped. I realized it was impregnable. I slowly backed up until I was about fifty feet from the wall and realized it only extended across the path. I had been blocked because I wasn't looking for alternatives; I was trying to bulldoze my way through. All I had to do was walk around the end of the wall and I was free. I awoke in jubilation.

This chapter describes alternatives to your blocks. These major obstacles to your success include outdated beliefs, conflicting desires, limited aspirations, lack of awareness, and fear of success. At first glance, the fear of success appears contradictory and highly unlikely, yet it is the most frequent block to having dreams come true.

## Release the fear of success

Is it possible that you fear success—to the extent you block future successes? The answer is yes. I learned this coaching a group of professionals and business people. Here were intelligent, highly functional people who were finding their dreams or desires blocked. They believed their successes were the result of luck and not skill. This placed their current achievements on very shaky ground; they wondered if they could retain their current position or ever achieve it again. Selectively using appropriate aptitude and ability tests, I was able to demonstrate rationally through their results that they hadn't just lucked into their success—it was something they had created using their skills. They could now accept that their fears were groundless, which allowed them to go on to create greater successes and fulfill bigger dreams.

Have you ever been excited about winning a lottery? You spend a few minutes dreaming of how you'll enjoy your windfall. Then, a thought occurs: "How will I handle all the requests for help?" Before you realize it, you start wondering if winning a lottery is a good thing or not. That's just one simple example of how you can begin to fear success. You become afraid that you will be unable to cope with the conditions that success brings. If you desire success in the entertainment world, your fears may involve coping with your fans and being perceived as public property. Success in any area usually means that people will continue to expect it from you. If you see your first success as a fluke and believe you will not be able to repeat it, then you fear that you will disappoint yourself and others.

So, the first step is to relax and accept that it's okay to have fear. Remember, if you start seeing your fear as a negative, something that shouldn't exist, it starts growing. Being afraid to deal with your fear does nothing but feed it. It is a paradox: fear is not to be feared, but to be made friends with. Imagine making friends with your fear! This is a different concept. But, the phrase "make friends with yourself" or "love yourself" includes your fear. The idea is extremely freeing. When you make friends with your fear, you are no longer held captive by it. Think about it: What is your fear telling you about yourself? What gift does it have to offer you? Once you know all about your fear, you can find ways to relieve any associated anxiety.

Now you are ready for the second step—expanding your vision to include this new insight into handling your fear. Judy and Randy, young, successful entrepreneurs, had not dealt with their fears when they created their visions for their businesses. Each was afraid that a successful business would mean too little free time. They each used their fear differently. Randy modified his vision to include hiring a business manager. Judy enrolled in a communications course to learn how to say no. This eased her fear about the demands she felt sure success would place on her. Fear needs only to be dealt with in a way that is acceptable to you. The answer does not lie in trying to find out *why* you have the fear. Searching for a why can take almost a lifetime and moves you no closer to the fulfillment of your desires. Instead, look for a way to deal with your fear so you can use it. Remember, you have created your desire and the accompanying fear, and you are accountable to yourself only.

When your vision is a full expression of you, the means to support it will appear. You can then thank your fear for alerting you to potential undesired situations. Know that having the ability to handle the changes is all part of your vision. You can deal with the concerns and there's nothing to fear—it's clear sailing. Return to seeing your dreams come true.

## Update your beliefs

Is it possible you're not blocked at all? You may be a person whose beliefs do not reflect your reality. Your life has changed over the course of time, yet a particular belief has not changed accordingly. For example, you believe that you don't have the means to live the way you desire. You believe you can't afford a long trip, a better car, or more luxurious housing. You may have developed this belief in your early years when you had very little money and lived frugally. You now have all the money and resources necessary to live as abundantly as you desire. Yet, if I were to suggest that you live abundantly, you would say you are blocked because of lack of funds. You truly believe that you don't have the money to live as you wish. You might reply, in all honesty, "I have to win the lottery before I can live that way." The problem really doesn't lie with a lack of funds but with your outdated beliefs. They are blocking you. The way around this block is to question yourself: "Do I really want to defer my desires in case some future catastrophe occurs, or do I want to live more assertively and in the present moment?" It also helps to ask, "How would I conduct my life if I had only a year to live?"

George needed to ask himself that question. He and his wife, Phyllis, had both taught school for more than twenty years while saving money and being frugal. Now in his mid-forties, George did not believe he had the necessary funds to do many of the things he and Phyllis desired. He claimed they had no money to renovate their house, buy a new car, or support their two sons in college. I asked him what he would do if he won a $200,000 lottery. He responded, "That would make a big difference, yet I have much more than that in savings and no debt." Contemplating that statement, George realized his beliefs had not kept pace with his abundance.

There are more examples of this type that occur when your belief system falls behind your personal growth. You have

---

**Exercise:** *Uncovering your growth*

1. Prepare a list detailing the capabilities and knowledge you have now that you didn't have ten years ago. This will take some time and effort and a great deal of honesty on your part. It's very easy to ignore your own accomplishments. For instance, in the last ten years you may have organized a multi-member household, or have managed a successful business. All the skills associated with these activities are ones you acquired during this period.

2. If you're having difficulty giving yourself this feedback, use the support group that was discussed in the previous chapter. You can ask three or four people who know you well (not family members or competitors) to function as your support group. Ask them to give you their perception of your abilities in relation to fulfilling your vision.

3. Use these lists to write a new belief that reflects this feedback. Repeat this new belief to yourself whenever the feeling of being blocked surfaces.

become more capable and developed many more resources than you recognize. Who you believe you are is outdated. You are still dragging along old beliefs from childhood or your early adult life. As usual, the answer to the block lies within you. Spend some time with yourself, get to know who you really are, and learn to appreciate your present capabilities. The exercise on the previous page will uncover your acquired skills and orient you to who you are now.

By focusing on a new belief, the old one will soon fade into oblivion. Before long, actually at the time the new belief becomes yours, you will find the blocks to your vision disappearing and your desires becoming part of your reality. The solution is awaiting your pursuit. Go for it!

## Clarify your desires

Do you really want it? I might ask you this question if you complained of a block. If your vision involves a new relationship, you might respond, "Why am I blocking a new relationship when I wish to have one?" The answer is simple. Change means moving into the unknown. The new situation is one you have not handled yet. The question you are really asking yourself, either openly or silently, is "Will I have to give up too much?" Sometimes the shift into the new is too threatening and so you block your vision. It also ties in with another question: "Is it worth relinquishing my independence for something I'm not sure I'm capable of handling?" You desire something new, yet maintain the status quo. It is important to realize you cannot hold on to your present situation; it is constantly in the process of creation and will not last.

You can reduce the threat of something new by experimenting slowly. When you go swimming, you don't have to plunge in immediately up to your neck. You can walk in leisurely and decide if you like the water. When new relationships are the concern, there is nothing wrong in telling potential partners that you are testing the waters. Explain to them that you enjoy your independence. Rather than damaging future prospects, this may enhance your situation. It is common knowledge that being too needy drives healthy, potential partners away. Being honest and open about your situation can make you more attractive than ever. There you go: a double-win situation for you.

This conflicting-desire block shows up in many situations. For example, you may desire a new wardrobe, and yet the change is not happening. Your closet is full of wonderfully familiar clothes; you feel that they are friends. It would be disloyal to give them away, and if not disloyal, at least wasteful. So here you are caught between two conflicting desires. The solution lies in determining what is more important to you, which desire you value most. Although this example is fairly straightforward and simplistic, many of your conflicting-desire challenges may appear more difficult to resolve.

For instance, you are experiencing frustration and dissatisfaction because you desire to spend more time with your family. Yet, to feel professionally fulfilled, you need to spend more time at work. You feel that both desires are in conflict and that they are mutually exclusive.

Step back for a moment and look at your challenge. What you may really desire is more satisfaction and harmony in dealing with two sets of demands. The answer may not lie in spending more time at work, or at home. When it becomes clear to you what desire to really focus on, solutions appear. You become creative. It may be possible to act so you respond to both demands at the same time. Can you work part of the week at home? Can you involve your family in your work? In a number of work situations, my family accompanied me to the office on weekends. My teenagers often helped me by manipulating data and researching the Web. Combining this tactic with working weekends gave us extra holidays. Another time, my daughter edited papers I was writing for university courses, giving us quality time together. In both cases I was spending more hours with my family without decreasing work time. You may also decide to change jobs in order to allow the two demands to be more inclusive. Recognizing your most heartfelt desire allows your creativity to flow. When you release your creativity on a challenge, you will be surprised how easily the appropriate solution appears.

## Enjoy your differences

Anything that you perceive as setting you apart from your friends or family introduces a potential block. This includes such changes as quitting smoking, buying a new car, taking a more positive attitude, modifying your eating habits, and moving to a community with a higher standard of living. As you express the new you, the transition makes you different.

Let's take an extreme case. Imagine being released from prison with a history of criminal activity. If you go straight, you will lose all your previous associates and friends who supported your crime and now feel a clear sense of betrayal. You will experience loneliness in the time space between where you are and where you want to be. Yet, this gap is necessary for you to progress. You really don't want conditions to remain the same or you wouldn't desire the change. The process requires some patience and appreciation of the possible opportunities that await you.

This block is caused by your need for approval. You are a social being and you have a need for social acceptance. The first step in removing this block is to accept your difference. The next step is to allow your support to come from a new source. You are on your own unique path. All along this path, a full set of resources emerges to support your growth. Like handrails on a staircase, these resources help you along, but as you go, you receive support from different spots on the railing. When you grasp the handrail firmly and refuse to let go, you become limited in your movement. It's like that on the path of life. If you always expect to receive support from the same spot on the path, you have to remain in the same place. Your movement ahead is restricted. To grow means you must loosen your grip on the old "handrail" and be open to accept new support as you progress. Look for help from those who are interested in growth and your evolution. These people are excited about what you are becoming and not what you were.

Slow down, take some deep breaths, and you will be surprised how fast you become aware of the support available to you. I offer this advice because I've experienced feelings of being unsupported that severely limited my awareness during times of change. My focus was on me and my perceived predicament. I had to learn to slow down and breathe. When I did, I became aware that all the support I needed was present and available. In one instance, I was living alone, having just separated from my wife. I felt deserted and unwanted. After a weekend of practising breathing and relaxation I was finally able to believe I would survive. At that point, I became aware of many who wanted to support me.

Long walks also help to bring me to the present moment and the necessary awareness of what truly exists. I strongly recommend walks outdoors for anyone experiencing acute stress. As the saying goes, it is a great life if we stay in the present moment. It's all there is, and that is all you and I need.

## Raise your sights

When you aim too low, you shoot yourself in the foot. It hurts and immobilizes you. This is what happens when you try to make changes that are not really changes. You're doing the same old thing, but dressing it up to look different. In this case, you are going to feel blocked and wonder what's going on—you will feel you are doing all the right things, but nothing is happening.

This limited-aspiration block haunted me over the course of a whole year. My vision included buying a multi-million-dollar business. I accomplished the first step by arranging all the financing including the necessary investors. Then problems kept interfering. At one point, the court awarded the desired business to a lower bidder; another time, the bank involved declared bankruptcy; and in the third deal, the vendor backed out. I became confused and perplexed. This time my support came from a colleague who suggested starting an entirely new company. This was a loftier, more ambitious goal than what I had planned originally. It meant I had to really raise my sights and accept the full challenge. Actually, that's what I had desired all along. The new venture was successful far beyond what

I'd hoped, and the lesson even more valuable.

If you seek change—not the same old thing dressed up in new clothes—go for what you truly want. Change means commitment; it means going all out. If you are blocked because you're underachieving, the block ultimately becomes a form of support. It affects you to such an extent that you cannot do the same old thing and call it change. Raising your ambition is a way of ensuring that your true desires are fulfilled.

When you're attempting something new and you keep getting rejected, check it out. Question yourself. "If my attempt succeeds, will I be satisfied? Will the result really feel like an achievement for me?" If the answers are no, then the solution to your block is to raise your sights, take an honest inventory of yourself and your abilities. Listen carefully to your heart's direction. A thought, an urge, a yearning will suggest what action you need to take next. It may mean pursuing the same goal, but using a different strategy to achieve it. It may also mean setting an entirely new goal and using a somewhat similar strategy to what you developed. In either case, you'll find the experience from the unsuccessful attempts will not be wasted. Furthermore, you'll find somewhere in your previous attempts you were underestimating yourself and what you could accomplish.

Look around. You will find there is support beyond yourself for the new adventure. It is time to shout, "Look out world, here I come!"

## Remove blind spots

Have you ever denied the existence of something in your life? This doesn't mean you have been lying to yourself or others. What it means is that you are unaware of something. Something is impacting on your life and causing unwanted consequences for you. A situation exists, or you're acting in a way that you are unable to acknowledge. Possibly, you are enabling someone to be dependent on you, or conversely, you are leaning on that person. In either case, growth is limited, and both of you will feel frustration. In the drama of your relationship, it is difficult to perceive any other script. This type of relationship can occur in many different settings—at work, in marriages, between parent and child—and can be recognized quite easily. The relationship is characterized when one member acts in a superior or dominant manner, and the other person is subservient or inferior. Usually both parties see their roles as necessary. There is no escape route; growth is inhibited. If you're seeking change, it is most effective to have a third-party observer. Depending on the situation, a management consultant, coach, or counselor can be very helpful in constructing a new relationship in which both members support and encourage growth in the other.

## Stop self-sabotage

Habitual negative, defeating self-talk is just as damaging as an addiction to drugs or alcohol. It is also a form of self-medication, since it dims your awareness and lessens the possibility of clear thinking. It is a way of avoiding problems. If you are unaware you practise this common habit, you won't realize how destructive it is. You won't know that you are sabotaging yourself with criticism and limiting messages. Common examples include: "I can't do that," "It is beyond my control," "I've failed again," and "It's no use."

If you are unaware of or deny this block, are you stuck? Not at all. This is where your support group can help. Look for someone who spends considerable time with you and believes in your potential. Ask them to monitor your speech for negative self-talk. After a day or two of observation, ask them to bring to your attention the negative statements you make about yourself. You can then take action to curb this self-defeating habit. Change "I can't" to "I can." Rephrase your negative self-talk so it becomes supportive. Change "I have no control over this" to "I am in control of myself, and I can take whatever action is necessary."

Don't expect just to stop your self-talk. Like everyone else, you always talk to yourself, either out loud or silently. So forget about stopping the habit; instead, change it. Be patient with yourself, because you've probably had years of practising the negative habit, and so it is unrealistic to expect to break it in days or weeks. Gaining awareness of what's going on is the first step to clearing this block to your growth.

You'll also want to examine the self-talk that goes on silently in your head. Make it a practice to stop several times a day and ask, "What was I thinking about?" When you focus on the subject, ask, "What was I telling myself about that? Was my self-talk helpful or limiting?" This line of questioning will give you insight to your silent conversations. The solution requires an honest assessment. You have no flaws or blemishes. You are a person of potential.

How do you know if you're learning and growing? It is a

positive sign if you're stumbling. If you're performing with-out errors or so-called mistakes, you're not learning. It means you are just repeating what you've learned already. Growth demands that you move on to something new. Be generous and forgiving of yourself in this arena of change. It is like learning how to speak a new language—you are going to make mistakes. Your errors in speech are not flaws in your person, but simply part of the process of learning. This process is true for other situations in your life. Give yourself some slack, and you will perform twice as well.

## Relax into change

Sometimes we try very hard and do everything we can think of to accomplish a goal, and nothing happens. Then it seems when we stop trying, we achieve our goal. One example, which has puzzled me, is childless couples who try for years to have children. Their dedication will take them to fertility clinics and other medical assistance, yet they remain child-less. Then they adopt a child. Shortly after, usually within one or two years, the woman becomes pregnant and they have their long awaited child. I know there are probable medical explanations for this phenomenon, yet it seems to deny a rational explanation. The process is similar to many other changes we desire in our life. We work to the point of being stressed at achieving some change and nothing hap-pens. It is only after we give up, relax, and almost forget about it, that the change happens.

Has this phenomenon ever happened to you? If you're feeling blocked, it can be happening again right now. You may have strongly desired some change for several months now and it has not happened. You're wondering why not, and you start questioning your ability and skill at achieving change. The answer doesn't seem to lie in your ability to create change. The explanation seems to be more in timing, or there is a more appropriate change waiting for you. It is not that the change or the desire is wrong. It is just that you benefit more if the change occurs later. This may sound like an irrational explanation, and it is. Yet, it always seems that after a period of time has passed, a very rational explanation is obvious to you.

One of the times I experienced this appearance of a block, I desired an acreage in the mountains. I followed all the prescribed steps I knew to manifest my desire. I drew pictures of the property, I used affirmations, and I visualized living on the land. It did not materialize—at least that's how it seemed to me. It wasn't until twelve years later, while driving into my driveway, that I realized my dream had been fulfilled. The gateposts were almost identical to the drawing I had made in my "vision picture" of the acreage. It had happened without my realization. Looking for an explanation, I discovered the delay was not caused by a lack of money. Instead, it was a lack of time. Owning the acreage any sooner would have been a burden to me, not a benefit. When I visualized the acreage, I wanted it to happen immediately so I would have proof that my vision could be manifested. But I would not have had the time or the mindset to enjoy it any earlier. Timing is an important consideration when it comes to change.

If nothing is happening, and it seems that you've gone through all the necessary steps to achieve your change, ask yourself, "Am I ready for this change; can I make full use of my desire if it's fulfilled right now?" If it appears to you that a later time would be better, relax and focus on something else. Probably the timing is not quite right. Enjoy what you are doing at the moment and give it your full attention. I'll bet that sometime in your future, your dream will come true, or something better will occur. You will be surprised how much the reality exceeds your expectations.

## Allow the shift

Blocks, you can see, are not always blocks. Often you have a deeper desire, of which you are unaware, because you will not allow yourself to dream it. This deeper desire requires modifying the change you are focusing on. When you're able to let go of the doubt and the anxiety of your initial desire, things happen. You start allowing parts of the "greater you" to surface. "What is the greater me?" you ask. It is the person that other people see, the person who is much more capable than you'll allow yourself to believe. So the secret for over-coming blocks does not lie in working harder into a state of stress and anxiety. Let go and believe in yourself. You then take action where and when obvious action is required.

If you are blocked by your tunnel vision and will not allow yourself to accept there are more effective actions, pause, breathe, stand back, and look at your challenge. A solution will become obvious as you allow life to provide what you request. Change is a magnificent process that I am still getting to know. May you enjoy it with me!

# Conclusion

Thank you for allowing me to share with you that change means opportunity. My clients, friends, and associates have been so generous in helping me to recognize this fact. They have helped me to experience the rhythm in life and to know there is an abundance of opportunities. These opportunities are always changing, always asking you to shift so that you can be more receptive and play your part in life's drama. You have a unique script to act out; you are simply encouraged to play an active part in writing it. You now have an outline and direction in how to develop the script and play your part.

You always were capable of living through change, but now you know how to master it. You are no longer at the whim of life; you are an active participant. You have found the ticket to make life an adventure. The wonderful part of it is you deserve it and you know how to enjoy it. You are capable of dealing with events as they occur in the present moment. By the present moment I mean right now—the only place where the action is. You have no need to delve into what could have been or what might be.

You have greater knowledge of fear, so it doesn't have to possess you. You can use your fear to energize you to accept the challenges that exist—challenges such as:

1. Living in the now.
2. Seeing alternatives in every situation.
3. Looking for beauty in your surroundings.
4. Appreciating skills learned from past events.
5. Being open to support from others.
6. Knowing you have worth.
7. Having no time or energy to be a victim.
8. Recognizing that every event or situation has a solution.
9. Perceiving new situations as challenges.
10. Caring for yourself because you have life and purpose.
11. Valuing everything in life, including pain.
12. Knowing change is inevitable.
13. Finding life an adventure.
14. Allowing change to come to you rather than trying to force it.
15. Owning your own fear.
16. Using your fear for creative means.
17. Feeling worthy without rescuing people.
18. Having no need to put others down to feel confident and competent.
19. Having no need to do everything yourself.
20. Observing and learning from your reactions to events.
21. Knowing that so-called failures are evidence that you are alive and learning.

No longer do you perceive success as an end point with you as the finished product. You know that you are in a constant state of becoming. I join you in the excitement of realizing we are dynamic beings, always changing and growing. As we experience each challenge, we have the potential to develop greater talents and beauty. And when we do, we are provided with more to share with the world. Life becomes a spiral rather than a straight line from start to finish. The more we grow, the more we have to offer. The more we offer ourselves to the world, the more we grow. And the spiral continues upwards. Join me in this incredible dance where change means the opportunity to create and relish a full life.

*To life!*

# Relevant Reading

*A Course In Miracles.* Glen Ellen, CA: Foundation for Inner Peace, 1976.

Bach, Richard. *Running from Safety.* New York: Morrow and Company, 1994.

Bridges, William. *Managing Transitions.* Reading, MA: Addison-Wesley, 1991.

Cameron, Julia. *The Vein of Gold.* New York: Tarcher/Putnam, 1996.

Casarjian, Robin. *Forgiveness.* New York: Bantam Books, 1992.

Chopra, Deepak. *How to Know God.* New York: Harmony Books, 2000.

Dyer, Wayne. *You'll See It When You Believe It.* New York: Morrow and Company, 1989.

Grabhorn, Lynn. *Excuse Me, Your Life is Waiting.* Olympia, WA: Beyond Books, 1999.

Hendricks, Gay. *Conscious Living.* Harper San Francisco, 2000.

Levine, Stephen. *A Year to Live.* New York: Bell Tower, 1997.

Mountain Dreamer, Oriah. *The Invitation.* Harper San Francisco, 1999.

Murphy, Joseph. *The Power of Your Subconscious Mind.* Englewood Cliffs, NJ: Prentice-Hall, 1963.

Pearsall, Paul. *Sexual Healing.* New York: Crown, 1994.

Redfield, James. *The Celestine Prophecy.* Hoover, AL: Satori, 1993.

Robbins, Anthony. *Awaken the Giant Within.* New York: Fireside, 1992.

Schachter-Shalomi, Zalman. *From Age-ing to Sage-ing.* New York: Warner, 1997.

Tolle, Eckhart. *The Power of Now.* Novato, CA.: New World Library, 1999.

Walsch, Neale. *Conversations with God, book 1.* New York: Putnam, 1996.

Wilde, Stuart. *Sixth Sense.* Carlsbad, CA: Hay House, 2000

## Author Contact

Hugh and Joanne Wiley offer seminars and workshops at which you can explore the changes you wish to make. The seminars cover the material in this book and much more. You will enjoy the fun, interactive style they have developed; you will leave the sessions feeling joyful and uplifted. You receive pre-seminar materials and use a workbook to record thoughts. Following the seminars, their support continues in the form of coaching to enhance your successful changes.

Currently they are traveling in the US and Canada, exploring the incredible variety of landscapes and diverse and interesting people they meet.

Use their web site **www.fulllifeseminars.com** to contact them or to verify when they will be in your region.

Copies of *Dancing with Change* can be ordered through your local bookstore or through the web site.